ADIRONDACK OUTLAWS

BAD BOYS AND LAWLESS LADIES

BY NIKI KOUROFSKY

FARCOUNTRY
PRESS

ISBN: 978-1-56037-611-8

© 2015 by Farcountry Press
Text © 2015 by Niki Kourofsky

Cover photographs courtesy of Library of Congress (Blue Mountain Lake),
National Archives, Atlanta (Eddie Collins), Plattsburgh Police Department
(Muskrat Robare), and Bloated Toe Enterprises (Jerry Blanch).

For more information about our books, write Farcountry Press, P.O. Box 5630, Helena, MT 59604;
call (800) 821-3874; or visit www.farcountrypress.com.

Library of Congress Cataloging-in-Publication Data

Kourofsky, Niki
  Adirondack outlaws : bad boys and lawless ladies / by Niki Kourofsky.
    pages cm
  Includes index.
  ISBN 978-1-56037-611-8 (pbk.)
  1. Crime--New York (State)--Adirondack Mountains--History. 2. Criminals--New York (State)--
Adirondack Mountains--Biography. 3. Adirondack Mountains (N.Y.)--Biography. I. Title.
  HV6793.N5K68 2015
  364.1092'27475--dc23
                                              2014037259

 Produced and printed in the United States of America.

25 24 23 22 21   2 3 4 5 6 7

TABLE OF CONTENTS

MURDERERS

UNSOLVED MYSTERIES

ACKNOWLEDGMENTS

Many thanks to Elizabeth Folwell, creative director of *Adirondack Life* magazine, for sharing her encyclopedic knowledge of the Adirondack region, and to the rest of the editorial crew—Annie Stoltie, Lisa Bramen, Kelly Hofschneider—for their unending support. Also thanks to Steven Engelhart, executive director of Adirondack Architectural Heritage; Hamilton County historian Bill Zullo; Town of Lake Pleasant historian Anne Weaver; Hilary "Guy" LeBlanc; Ray Smith; Town of Thurman historian Joan Harris; Persis Granger; Marilyn Van Dyke, research center chair at the Warren County Historical Society; the staff of the Adirondack History Center Museum; Jerold Pepper, Adirondack Museum library director; David Starbuck; Larry Gooley; Captain Michael Branch and Detective Edward Smith, Plattsburgh City Police Department; Kristy Rubyor, Town of Webb Historical Association; Town of Webb historian Peg Masters; Rod Bigelow; Cathy Miller, National Archives at Atlanta; the Lake Placid Police Department; and the long-suffering research assistants at the New York State Archives. And thank you to my children, Alex and Ailyn, for their patience, and to my very favorite scofflaw, Derry Staley. ⇥

INTRODUCTION: FOREVER WILD

It's impossible to introduce a cast of Adirondack characters without first painting the backdrop—though, mind you, I'm just splashing around a little color. A pilgrim can spend years wandering the wilderness of this region's history and emerge no wiser than when she began. Still, I can give you the Cliff's Notes.

When a crew of privileged men got together in 1892 to lasso the great and wild Adirondacks within a blue border (a color choice that added "Blue Line" to our regional lexicon), they weren't just creating a one-of-a-kind state park; they were also birthing a tangled mess. The now six-million-acre conservation experiment is a mash-up of public and private land, a melting pot—and, sometimes, a seething caldron—of differing needs and wants, philosophies and prejudices. And it all teeters on that founding paradox: an attempt to preserve an untamed landscape by taming it.

Why did they even try? Did the impulse emerge from a desire to recalibrate society's dysfunctional relationship with the natural world? Not really. The politicians' protective instincts had a bit more to do with another kind of green: the Benjamins.

By the middle of the nineteenth century, and especially after the Civil War, travelers were falling in love with the romantic Adirondacks—a fantasyland blanketed by thick forest and dotted with sparkling lakes and sky-scraping mountains. (There were also roughhewn communities with farms and mills and struggling settlers, though those scenes didn't enter into the purple prose of early travel writers.) Although he was hardly the first to extoll its virtues, William H. H. "Adirondack" Murray is credited for putting the tourist stampede on steroids with his 1869 smash hit *Adventures in the Wilderness; or, Camp-Life in the Adirondacks*. Murray's chronicle

A stagecoach brings guests to a grand hotel on Blue Mountain Lake.
PHOTOGRAPHY BY SENECA RAY STODDARD, COURTESY LIBRARY OF CONGRESS, LC-USZ62-74950.

cemented the place's reputation as a sporting paradise, with its "pure, rari-
fied, and bracing" air acting as a curative for body and soul. (His spectacularly unprepared disciples who raced higgledy-piggledy to the woods were
dubbed "Murray's Fools.") Fashionable hotels like the Prospect House, in
Blue Mountain Lake, and Paul Smith's resort, on Lower St. Regis Lake,
sprouted up around the area, giving well-heeled visitors the opportunity
to enjoy the natural world within a properly curated setting. More out-
doorsy types rented backcountry-savvy servants to guide them to the best
hunting and fishing spots—and build their shelters, and carry their gear,
and cook their dinners. Those with enough means to fully remove themselves from the common rabble built cloistered palaces that they referred
to as "camps."

The region was an unspoiled wonder, Murray rhapsodized, where the
"forest stands as it has stood, from the beginning of time, in all its majesty
of growth, in all the beauty of its unshorn foliage." But with its vast acres

Established in 1892, Adirondack Park preserves 6 million acres of high peaks, boreal forests, and pristine waterways. PHOTOGRAPH BY WILLIAM HENRY JACKSON, COURTESY LIBRARY OF CONGRESS, LC-DIG-DET-4A16959.

of timber and rich veins of ore, the Adirondacks couldn't escape exploitation forever. Its vulnerability made wealthy visitors nervous for the future of their playground and also worried business concerns, who argued that upstate clear-cutting would wreak havoc with water levels in the Hudson River and Erie Canal. In the end, it was the threat to commerce rather than the threat to nature that held more sway in the New York State Legislature.

So baby steps were taken to protect this Garden of Eden from our baser instincts. The Adirondack Forest Preserve was created in 1885, a move that still made allowances for responsible logging on state tracts. (The state had unwittingly become a large stakeholder in Adirondack land, thanks in part to logging companies abandoning tracts they no longer considered profitable.) But what constituted responsible logging was left up to the Forest Commission, which was also tasked with feathering the state treasury. The whole situation smacked of the fox guarding the henhouse.

In 1890, the state signaled that it was interested in expanding its Adirondack landholdings beyond the leavings of the lumber companies, and in 1892 the Adirondack Park was born—though not yet fully conceived. Three years later, park protections were strengthened by the adoption of Article VII (now XIV) of the New York State Constitution: "The lands of the state, now owned or hereafter acquired, constituting the forest preserve as now fixed by law, shall be forever kept as wild forest lands." But when it came to considering the fate of private holdings within the Blue Line or the needs of year-round residents, those cans were kicked down the trail. The first question was finally addressed when the Adirondack Park Agency was created in 1971 to oversee state tracts and regulate development on private land. As far as the second sticking point—well, the natives didn't exactly embrace the new bureau as a champion of their needs.

For all the passion and poetry it incites, this landscape has always been a tough place to scratch out a living. And the rules that outsiders cooked up to dictate how settlers could make it work were taken—or not—on a case-by-case basis. Like many other Adirondackers whose roots go back a few generations, I come from a family of outlaws. Most settlers around here didn't worry too much over game laws when taking a deer meant feeding your family. And if setting up a still took the edge off risking life and limb in a mine for barely enough to survive, the disapproval of the revenue man didn't carry a lot of weight.

But the outlaws on the following pages aren't your garden variety Adirondack scofflaws and scallywags—the majority of them weren't even locals. Alongside the tourists and the robber barons, certain criminal elements found a lot to like about the North Woods, with its isolated towns and dark recesses. And its handy location just a holler from the Canadian border, that was pure gravy.

Before the Adirondack Park was even a twinkle in a politician's eye, Big James Brady, a slick safecracker from down Albany way, found an ideal mark resting on the banks of the region's mighty Ausable River. Keeseville was a bustling industrial center, at least by North Country standards, with tidy sums passing through its snug little bank. But it was still a backwater, and after Brady and his gang subdued the night watchmen at the factory across the street, there was no one left around to gainsay them.

Some spots around the region were isolated in more than one way. In the boom years of Adirondack industry, railroad, mining, and logging concerns trucked in immigrants to do most of the heavy lifting. And in company towns, workers tended to sort themselves into ethnic enclaves. The residents of Lyon Mountain, a tiny mining community in the very northern reaches of the park, still refer to sections of town as "Pollack Hill" or "Sweden." Since those little communities-within-communities were cut off by language barriers and suspicion of outside authority, folks fresh off the boat were vulnerable to abuse. Gangs like the "Black Hand," unaffiliated bands of Mafia wannabes, had little trouble shaking down newcomers.

For those who knew how to unlock its secrets, the backcountry could offer outlaws the upper hand, allowing fugitives to outsmart posses for days (Charles Parker, 1881; Sam Pasco, 1918), or months (James Call, 1954), or even forever (the North River stage bandit, 1901). But the region's nooks and crannies also made excellent staging grounds for illicit enterprises. The "Windfall" section of Wells, a particularly remote stretch of wilderness, acted as a home base for the notorious Wadsworth clan and a hidey-hole for their stolen goods. (Around here, a "windfall" isn't a stroke of good luck; it's a swath of forest snarled by an epic windstorm.) "Canton" Eddie Collins and his pals found the perfect place to set up shop around 1907—a tramp camp by the train tracks a bit north of the Adirondack Park. At the border town of Rouses Point, a fluid cast of characters had plenty of privacy and access to easy traveling around upstate New York and into Canada.

Natives and visitors benefited from the region's prime real estate when Prohibition came along. Both Route 9, which shot down the Champlain Valley to Albany, and Route 22, running through West Chazy to Plattsburgh, became major hooch highways, but the trade also snaked along Routes 9N and 3. Quiet country roads turned into exciting race tracks—or demolition derbies—as bootleggers and bluecoats played fast-paced games of keep-away. Spectators were generally on the side of the runners. In *Rum Across the Border,* Allen Everest described one North Hudson liquor bust that left a couple of state troopers red-faced—they were surrounded by a mob who managed to liberate the shipment. Sometimes Volstead violators turned on each other, robbing competing couriers or, in the case of Mystery Montague, holding up a speakeasy for a quick wad of dough. Prohibition made for high times in the area, but when it was over, at least one big leaguer didn't know what to do with himself. Charles "Muskrat" Robare turned to cattle rustling, then to murder.

It wasn't just bootleggers that some locals aided and abetted. In 1917, a New York State police force was formed to patrol and protect rural pockets of the state. Except the residents of those rural pockets weren't so sure they wanted the protection of outsiders. That was made pretty clear a year later, when the newly minted state troopers were tasked with running down the Thurman murderer Sam Pasco. Although there was no question of his guilt, native son Pasco got more help in hiding than the troopers got in their search.

Local prejudices also worked in favor of a still-unnamed killer when land baron Orrando Dexter was gunned down in the town of Waverly in 1903. The relationship between year-round Adirondackers and the tourists and second-homers they served had always been a bit prickly. On the one hand, locals needed the cash the locusts brought; on the other, the city slickers needed the hard work and expertise of the natives. But between the two groups there was sometimes suspicion, and very often a healthy dose of contempt, on both sides of the exchange. Dexter brought this subtext to the surface when he barreled into the area, scooped up a bunch of property, then told everyone who had ever worked, fished, or hunted on his land to go get bent. It didn't end well for him.

You might notice that two of the Adirondacks' most famous villains do not appear in this volume: Chester Gillette, who murdered his pregnant girlfriend by knocking her into Big Moose Lake with a tennis racket in 1906, and Robert Garrow, the serial rapist and killer who murdered three Adirondack tourists in 1973. But so much ink has been spilled over those two vermin that I'm sure there's nothing more I can add.

I chose the desperados that are profiled here for their entertainment value, leaning toward lively yarns of derring-do—and since murder doesn't fall into that category, I would have loved to avoid it altogether. But the savage stories that did creep into these chapters had elements that made the tales worth telling: Debosnys was a fascinating nineteenth-century nut job. Sam Pasco still enjoys a certain folk-hero status in pockets of the park.

Muskrat Robare started out as a rock star of the regional bootlegging scene. Ernest Duane is said to have mourned his cancelled chicken dinner when he was saved from the electric chair in 1930. And the manhunt for Major James Call was the longest in Adirondack history.

But I'd like to take a moment to remember their victims: Betsey Wells, an enterprising mother of four daughters; Orlie Eldridge, a hardworking farmer and father of seven; Yale Morris, a successful immigrant whose murder may have had as much to do with his Jewish faith as with the cash in his pocket; Eula Davis, a loveable backwoods guide and caretaker; Patrolman Richard Pelkey, a 31-year-old husband and father who was shot while protecting his community. And Orrando Dexter.

One final note: The phrase "Blue Line," referring to the border of the Adirondack Park, is thrown around so much it seems more like a physical barrier than a political construct. But it's not—there's no gatehouse at the park entrance—and the line itself has been expanded a number of times over the years. "Adirondack" crimes detailed in this book may have occurred before there was an Adirondack Park, or in an Adirondack community before it technically joined the Adirondack Park, or even outside the modern boundary. To make everything a bit easier on all of us, when I describe a location's position in, out, or around the Adirondack Park, I use the current Blue Line as reference. ↠

ADIRONDACK PARK

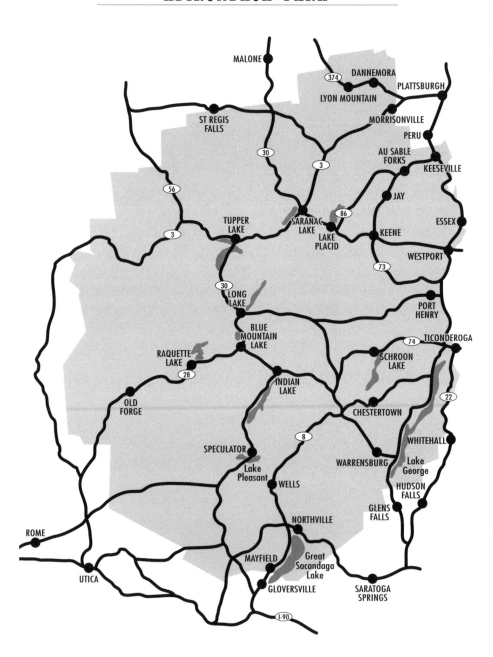

CHAPTER ONE

Safecrackers, Sneak Thieves, and Stickup Men

THE BRADY BUNCH

"Brady's career is one of an extraordinary character, and his latest exploit is nothing more than was expected of him by the officers and attachés of the criminal courts acquainted with his desperate character and fertility of resource when in difficulty."

—*New York Times*, October 21, 1873

The jig could have been up after the first muffled explosion echoed through the sleepy village of Keeseville. But the only people around to raise the alarm—Henry Duval, John Collins, and William Ames— were a bit indisposed. As the Keeseville National Bank was being ransacked in the wee hours of July 7, 1877, the trio was trussed up across the road, at the headquarters of the Ausable Horse Nail Company.

Duval, a watchman for the nail company, had been set upon by three men in white masks as he returned from his midnight rounds. His attackers were taking no chances with the imposing Civil War veteran— he was roughed up and disarmed, his hands clamped into iron cuffs and a handkerchief jammed in his mouth. Upstairs, Collins, another employee of the works, was being dragged out of his bunk by a second group of three. Duval and Collins were blindfolded and bound to chairs on the upper story, their feet locked down by heavy straps screwed to the floor.

Moments later, their coworker Ames was startled by a banging on the door of the watch-house, where he was passing the time sorting nails. Ames said he thought it was "some of the boys just returning from fishing." Instead, three armed men snatched up the elderly keeper and secured him on the second floor with the others. The gunmen then demanded the key to the bank, which was in Duval's keeping. He played dumb only once— a pistol butt to the skull quickly convinced him to give up the goods.

Five more muted explosions followed the first, then silence. Around three in the morning, the roughneck who'd stayed behind to babysit the prisoners took his leave. The men began to holler at the first stirrings of morning—the rumble of the four o'clock stage to Port Kent—but the driver couldn't hear the commotion through the nail company's two-foot-thick stone walls. So the men improvised: Collins dragged himself across the floor and unfastened Ames's bindings with his teeth.

Once free, Collins ran to notify the bank cashier and Duval raced to the bank. The place was billowing with so much blue smoke that Duval could hardly see. "It had a sickish smell," he later reported. "[It] did not smell like powder." When the smoke settled, Duval found the Marvin "burglar-proof" safe blown open and cleaned out—the bank took a hit for about $7,000 in cash, $70,000 in bonds, and $160,000 in notes. Some of the crooks' tools were left behind: an eight-inch steel punch and steel wedge, a square bellows, and a piece of fuse.

That blue smoke and sickish smell were hallmarks of nitroglycerin, a more sophisticated safe buster than gunpowder. The *Plattsburgh Sentinel* speculated that the break-in marked "the first time in the history of burglaries" that the powerful liquid was used. That's unlikely. But the gang of at least six, maybe ten, was definitely at the forefront of their field, well organized and well outfitted. They were professionals—and they were gone.

Rumors flew as bank agents piled into the tiny Champlain Valley community. The *Plattsburgh Republican* broke the story that the robbers had been spotted at Chateaugay Lake the next day, forty-some miles north, but that was the last whisper of their whereabouts until late August. That's when a package from Albany appeared in town, stuffed with the

Nightwatchmen for the Ausable Horse Nail Company were tied up on the second floor of the factory (left) while James Brady and his bunch cleaned out the Keeseville National Bank across the road. PHOTOGRAPH BY G. F. MARVIN, COURTESY OF ADIRONDACK ARCHITECTURAL HERITAGE.

stolen notes and a polite missive to the bank president: "We send this for the reason we cannot use it ourselves. This is all you need expect to get, as the rest is all sold and spent. You can hire all the detectives in America, and you will be no nearer than you were before you started; you will only be so much out."

The gang's boasting was a bit premature. Authorities had, in fact, just nabbed a prime suspect: Oscar D. Peterson, also known as James Brady or Albany Jim (he hailed from the Capitol Region). Brady ran with a who's who of late nineteenth-century scofflaws—Big Frank McCoy, John "Red" Leary, Dan Noble, "Shang" Draper. The *New York Times* called him one of the most "scientific burglars," an expert with explosions who could blow open a vault without waking the neighborhood.

Brady paid his dues in the minor leagues—dabbling in forgery and making the papers in 1865 for a violent robbery near Albany—but during his lengthy career he was linked to some of the most notorious bank break-ins of the time. One was the 1869 Ocean Bank job in New York City, where he and his confederates rented space in the bank's basement and tunneled up through the floor. The *Troy Times* estimated that the take was $400,000, though the *New York Times* put it closer to a million. For a comparatively smaller $60,000 heist at the Orchard Street Savings Bank in Philadelphia, in 1870, Brady's bunch passed themselves off as cops to gain access to the vault after hours. But they really outdid themselves in Massachusetts in 1876, holding a clerk and his family hostage while relieving Northampton National Bank of more than a million dollars. Brady wasn't tried for any of those monkeyshines—except in the press, where he was convicted of being a dashing criminal mastermind. He was equally famous for jail breaks, giving turnkeys the slip three times in little more than a year.

The Keeseville caper wasn't Brady's first visit to the Adirondack region. Back in 1870, before he'd graduated to nitro, Albany Jim and his pals pried open the backdoor of the Glens Falls National Bank and used gunpowder to demolish the vault. Around three in the morning a clerk from a neighboring shop heard the booms, though he was too busy cowering in fear to alert the cops. When the bank opened, workers found bits of papers and cash littering the floor, many of the bills burned to bits. The theft totaled around $18,000 in cash and $6,000 in government bonds.

Investigators discovered that five well-dressed strangers with a team of ponies and a jaunty black-and-yellow wagon had been spotted around Saratoga. The crew—"looking like first-class blacklegs," according to the *Troy Times*—changed out their horses at a local livery just before the break-in and returned the loaners the morning after. The next day an envelope with a somewhat scorched will from the Glens Falls bank was found on the streets of Albany. That was the only trace anyone found of the loot—until three years later.

In May 1873, when Brady was on the lam from Auburn Prison (he'd been doing time for a $6,000 score from a New York City optician's office), he was nabbed trying to fence $30,000 of bonds at the offices of a phony doctor. Detectives hauled him in—after another desperate escape attempt involving a jump from a second-floor window—and discovered

Glens Falls bank bonds among Brady's cache. He was given three and a half years at Sing Sing; after that stint, he'd have to serve the remainder of his sentence in Auburn.

Even the formidable walls of Sing Sing couldn't hold Albany Jim. In October of 1873, one of Brady's buddies on the outside slipped him some tools and, during a thunderstorm, he and his cellmate made their break. They hoodwinked the guard with a couple of dummies under their blankets and opened their cell, easy as you please, with a false key. Then they forced the window bars open with a jackscrew and lowered themselves into the yard on a rope of blanket strips.

Brady was off and running—straight to his next job, a month later at the First National Bank of Wilmington, in Delaware. But that break-in backfired when one of the gang's hostages escaped and called in the cops. Brady and his pals were given forty lashes in a public square and sentenced to ten years in prison. Brady took his lickings but didn't bother with the jail time. He and his mates escaped almost as soon as the cell doors slammed shut behind them.

Brady may have been a master safecracker and escape artist, but he wasn't very good at blending in. By all accounts he was a big man, tall and powerfully built, and partial to fancy clothes. About a month after the Keeseville job, the dapper crook—"flashily dressed" with "flowing whiskers," reported the *New York Times*—wandered into Ward's Furnishing Store and pocketed about $20 worth of silk handkerchiefs and other fripperies right under the clerk's nose. The outraged clerk complained to a policeman, who rounded Brady up and took him back to the store for a positive ID.

Confronted by his accuser, Brady countered, "My dear fellow, you must be wrong." But he couldn't explain away the stolen goods in his pockets. As the officer escorted the red-handed robber toward the stationhouse, Brady pulled out his Derringer and sprinted through the crowded streets. A pack of police was soon on his tail, but Brady wasn't going down without a fight. He shot wildly at his pursuers—one in a commandeered wagon—and even lobbed an umbrella into the fray. He landed two shots, one grazing an officer and the other wounding a waiter who had joined in the chase. (Neither suffered much: the cop walked away with a bruised ego, and the over-eager citizen was healthy enough to testify at Brady's trial, just a month later.)

When he was finally collared, the *New York Times* wrote that officers found a cool $1,300 on him, plus a "vial of mysterious liquid and curious shaped keys." Suspecting they had a big-time player in their grasp, authorities called in detectives and the deputy warden from Sing Sing. In the meantime Brady convinced his gullible guards to let him slip into plain clothes, cut his hair and shave off his whiskers. His quick-change routine might have confused the average witness, but Brady's old acquaintance from Sing Sing easily identified him.

He was never tried for the Keeseville caper—although it was credited to him in the press—but that $20 theft and bullet-strewn chase were raps Brady couldn't escape. For the shooting of Edward Bromfield, the waiter who got in his way, Brady was sentenced to eleven years in Auburn, with his unexpired term of six and a half years tacked on afterward. And this time he finally did his time. After his release, he spent the next decade or so out of major trouble—or at least out of the spotlight.

He made the news again in 1900, though his situation was more pauper than prince of thieves. Papers from as far away as Toronto wrote that the seventy-some-year-old Brady was found in a Westchester County barn "starving and dying of chills and fever . . . like a hunted, friendless thing." But he wasn't completely without friends. Neighbors brought the broken man to the hospital, where Brady regained enough strength to linger a while longer.

When he was first found shivering and near death, he told his rescuers that "the criminal is a fool." But with a warm bed at the Westchester County poorhouse and a rapt audience, his tune changed a bit. He held court with reporters, happily recounting his past exploits and top-shelf lifestyle (he had lived large at a New Rochelle estate during his days of wine and roses). Brady told the *New York Herald* that he didn't think much of his current accommodations. Gesturing to the window, he said, "Mebbe I'll get out there again sometime."

Brady did make it out in May of 1903, when he said his final goodbyes at the almshouse and took off "he knew not whither," according to the *New Rochelle Pioneer*. Where he ended up was dodging trains down at the tracks. He managed to evade one express, but only by jumping into the path of another—and the business end of a locomotive was one authority even old Albany Jim couldn't escape. ⇥

How to Crack a Safe

Well-outfitted gangs of the late nineteenth century had plenty of toys for prying open a safe—compound jimmies, steel wedges, jackscrews. But for the less patient burglar, there was always gunpowder: bore a hole in the lock, stuff some powder in, and set it off. Allan Pinkerton, founder of the Pinkerton Detective Agency—which became as infamous as the criminals it hunted—wrote in *Thirty Years a Detective* (1884) that another way to blow a vault "is to putty up all the crevasses of the safe compactly except at two points. At one of these points the air pump is applied, which exhausts the air within the safe, and at the other point the powder is drawn in by the force of the suction." When the charge is lit, the explosion will take a door from its hinges.

James Brady was a bit ahead of his time, foregoing powder and drills for newfangled nitroglycerin. In 1904, William A. Pinkerton, Allan's son, explained the use of nitro in *The Yeggman: Bank Vault and Safe Burglar of Today.* ("Yegg" was early twentieth-century slang for safecracker.) Modern burglars, he explained, "seal up the cracks of vault or safe doors with common washing soap, well softened, leaving a slight aperture at top of door where a soap dam is built into which the 'soup' or nitro-glycerine is poured. This oozes about cracks of safe very quickly; a fuse and detonator are used to explode it." One post office inspector of the time noted that Naptha soap was a bad-boy favorite, because it "kneaded well."

CHAPTER TWO

Safecrackers, Sneak Thieves, and Stickup Men

"CANTON" EDDIE COLLINS

*"Collins has had a spectacular career. His episode at
Lake Placid involved the use of a boat in which he made
his getaway across Mirror Lake after blowing the safe. . . .
'Canton Eddie' has been called the 'brainiest of crooks.'"*

—*Essex County Republican,* May 14, 1915

A t about two in the morning on May 18, 1911, neighbors of H. J. Bull's Saranac general store—and even Mr. Bull's daughter—were jolted awake by booming explosions, though no one bothered to get out of bed and investigate. If the residents of this woodsy northern Adirondack town had been a little more curious, they might have stumbled across a couple of strangers cleaning out the post office safe in the back of Bull's shop. The burglars had smashed the place's windows—another ruckus that failed to roust the natives—once they realized they couldn't jimmy the door with a chisel stolen from the local wheelwright. The pair's work on the safe was just as subtle: the vault was blown apart in three powerful blasts that blanketed the office with books and papers.

The theft wasn't discovered until after daybreak, when a local horse trainer trotted by and noticed the broken glass. So the trail was pretty cold by the time Clinton County Sheriff Mark Tierney and Plattsburgh Police Chief Andrew Connors raced to the scene. They followed two sets of footprints five miles to Cadyville, but lost the tracks near Gougeville spring, where the dirt gave way to macadam. The culprits got away with about $100 in cash, $1,000 in checks, and a pile of postage stamps.

Could this have been the work of Canton Eddie, a native of St. Lawrence County and the North Country's most prolific safecracker? Maybe. Eddie, under the name Edward Collins, had been released from federal prison in Atlanta in March. Since he wasn't picked up again until June—in Utica, for vagrancy—Eddie might have had the opportunity to breeze through Saranac, a couple hundred miles to the northeast.

But busted windows, borrowed tools, over-the-top explosions, escaping on foot? None of it was Eddie's style.

Edward Collins, alias Edward Burns, Edward Barnes, Edward Wilson, Harold Wilson, aka Canton Eddie, started life around 1872 in the little town of Canton, just outside the northwest border of the modern Adirondack Park. As a young man, he was a "bad one," according to the *Auburn Democrat Argus*, with a mother to match. After some time in a Rochester reform school, Eddie ran off with the circus, working as a hostler and falling in with the seedy drifters who trailed traveling carnivals. He did short stints in slammers in the Albany area, but graduated to hard time in 1897, when he netted three and a half years in Dannemora's Clinton Prison for grand larceny.

After his time in Dannemora, nicknamed "Little Siberia," and a one-year detour to an Ohio penitentiary, Eddie started his career proper. Around 1904, Eddie was working the outskirts of the Adirondack region, hitting depots and post offices along the Rome, Watertown & Ogdensburg Railroad line, with a few forays back into St. Lawrence County. "He was chased all over the state," wrote the *Democrat Argus*, "but he managed to elude officers." By 1907, he'd settled on a base of operations to the northeast, spending his summers with fellow yeggmen at a tramp camp near the rails in Rouses Point. The outpost was at the tippy-top of New York State, convenient to both Canada and backwater Adirondack towns.

In November of that year, Eddie's Rouses Point gang hit a store in nearby Mooers Forks, then hopped across the border to snatch some cash from a bank in Napierville, Quebec. They used two blasts of nitro to break the safe after the manager refused to cooperate. The bandits escaped on a handcar with $2,000 in cash; the manager escaped with some bruises about the head.

In January 1908, Eddie's winning streak came to an end when he and his tall friend Joseph "Toad" Thornton were busted for a post office job in Port Byron, near Auburn, that netted a measly $205.96 in stamps and about four dollars in pennies. The pair was collared a few days later, thanks to a clumsy attempt to sell some discount stamps in a Lyons barroom, plus an eyewitness who spotted "a long and a short man" fleeing the scene. Authorities found revolvers and a safecracking kit on the suspects.

At first, officers couldn't place Toad's partner—a John Doe in a bowler hat with deep-set eyes, a short mustache, and a less-than-impressive stature—but an ex-sheriff from St. Lawrence County helped solve the mystery. Despite some vanishing evidence and a sketchy hobo as witness for the prosecution, the dynamic duo were sentenced to four years hard labor in Auburn Prison. (It didn't help their case when a shopkeeper testified that the defendants' court clothes had been stolen from his store.) Eddie was later transferred to the federal prison in Georgia; he was out by 1911, when he may or may not have hit Mr. Bull's store in Saranac.

It definitely was Eddie who showed up in Syracuse in September of that year with what the *Ogdensburg News* described as enough nitroglycerin to "blow up an army." He and his buddy were nailed with a bottle of the explosive, five saws, and a razor, plus caps, fuses, and $152 in cash. Detectives tried to connect him to a slew of safe burglaries around the area, but they came up empty. Eddie did an easy six months in jail for holding burglar's tools.

He went straight back to his old ways after his release. In 1912, the *Ticonderoga Sentinel* fingered him for plundering "upwards of thirty post office safes in New York State in the last year," calling northern New York—especially around the Black River Railroad and the St. Lawrence River Valley—his "favorite field for safe blowing." But Eddie really made a name for himself that May for his Houdini-like escape near Rome, New York.

Railroad detectives had been out netting their quota of stowaways outside Verona one night when two men jumped off the freight train and ran for the hills. They didn't stop until "the officers were obliged to use their revolvers," according to the *Ogdensburg Journal*. The dicks found a little over $100 in cash on the alleged hobos, as well as fuses and caps, some soap, nitroglycerin, and a few revolvers. Eddie was sporting his signature black derby.

The pair was dragged into the Verona station with the rest of the transients and handcuffed to the railing. But as soon as the officers left to bring in another batch of freeloaders, Eddie broke his bonds and melted into the night. Although he had given his name as John Burns, Canton Eddie wasn't fooling anyone. He was, proclaimed the *Ogdensburg Journal*, "one of the best known crooks in the East." Police speculated that he and his partner were on the run from a recent post office robbery about forty miles to the west.

It was in peaceful Lake Placid, in the heart of the Adirondack Mountains, where Eddie may have pulled off his classiest caper. In the early morning hours of June 7, 1912, a slick burglar rowed across Mirror Lake, levered the post office window open, wrapped the safe in wet blankets—an Eddie signature—and blew it open without waking a man sleeping a couple dozen feet away. He rowed back with about $3,000 in loot and motored out of the area in an automobile. The *Ticonderoga Sentinel* reported that the heist was "laid at Collins' door by police officials who have watched the career of the prolific operator on big safes."

Having a car handy for a quick getaway was another hallmark of Eddie's jobs. In the fall of 1912, the *Plattsburgh Sentinel* wrote that Eddie "uses a high power automobile" and was most likely responsible for the "epidemic" of auto-aided robberies throughout the region. The next year, when a post office was hit in the southern Adirondacks, the *Amsterdam Evening Recorder* fingered Eddie as the perp, assuring readers that "the job looks like another one which 'Canton Eddie' Collins is pulling off . . . the mysterious yeggman who travels in a high power motor car, cracking POs about the country."

By this time the feds had a pretty sweet price on Eddie's head and Pinkerton detectives were on his trail. When he was finally nabbed in Syracuse in May of 1915—again for storing enough nitroglycerin to make an earth-shattering kaboom—a front-page headline for the *Essex County*

Republican proclaimed that the "Lake Placid Safe Blower is Captured." The article explained that, although he had grown a beard, "his sharp, rat-like eyes betrayed him."

Eddie protested that he and his pal were in town on a drinking spree and that he was "clean." He did have soap and towels on him, though arresting officers surely knew it wasn't good hygiene that Eddie was practicing. The cops also found a well-thumbed book that listed New York post offices and a map of the railroad system. But more damning was the package a local bartender coughed up, confessing that Eddie had asked him to hold the stash of fuses and caps, an electric light, revolvers and ammo, two chisels, some keys, and a quart bottle of concentrated nitro-glycerin—"enough to blow up the largest building in the city," according to the *Syracuse Daily Journal.* Authorities assumed that it was Eddie and his partner who'd recently snatched fifty pounds of dynamite from an Auburn quarry. The *Journal* reported that the culprits were tracked to a culvert, "where the men had boiled the dynamite to extract the nitro glycerin. The tin cans in which the operation had been performed, two unused sticks of the explosive, and an old bandana handkerchief which had been used as a strainer for the stuff were also picked up."

Prosecutors threw everything they could at Eddie and none of it stuck. He pleaded guilty to possessing a revolver at his arrest back in Verona and was sentenced to one year and eight months in Auburn Prison.

Eddie was out and running by 1917, when he was caught up in a botched railroad-station job in western New York with a ne'er-do-well from Old Forge. Once he was back in chains, it was the usual routine: detectives scrambled to link him to all manner of thievery across the region. Eddie managed to skate out of everything. And since it was one of his companions who was actually carrying the tools of the trade—fuses, caps, revolvers—authorities couldn't nail Eddie for that, either. So prosecutors slapped the aging crook with the only thing they could, a charge of vagrancy that netted him 180 days in jail. At his sentencing, he promised the judge he was done with crime, saying, "I'm 45 years old and all shot to pieces. . . . I am going straight for there is nothing in the game any more." Besides, he complained, "every time a safe is cracked from Maine to California . . . they blame it on Canton Eddie."

The Bertillon identification card from "Canton" Eddie Collins's time in the federal pen at Atlanta, 1909. COURTESY OF NATIONAL ARCHIVES AT ATLANTA.

But his brushes with the law weren't over. In early 1919, an impoverished-looking Eddie resurfaced in Buffalo with a bullet lodged above his heart. The *Buffalo Courier* had a good time at his expense, pointing out his "lady-like fingers" and noting that if he'd hit any safes lately, "he didn't spend coin on clothes." Eddie was mild-mannered and generally cooperative, though he refused to say who shot him or why, or even where it happened. He protested he "was not contemplating anything unlawful when wounded." Even so, he was paraded in front of police from all precincts. "Everybody had a good look," the *Courier* wrote, "but that did not help prove any case in city court, and the prisoner was turned loose." Their front-page headline closed the curtain on a storied career: "Canton Eddie, Suave, Secretive, Departs." ⇥

How Yeggs Operate

Turn-of-the-century safecrackers, or "yeggs," often set up shop in isolated tramp camps—one of Canton Eddie's naughty-boy nests was by the Rutland Railroad line in Rouses Point. The gang would send out feelers, usually innocent-looking boys, to recon targets in quiet rural communities. These "Gay Cats," as they were known, took note of everything: police or watchmen, streetlights, bank entrances, safe models, train schedules. Then, on a moonless night, the talent would hop into town for a quick score.

One of Eddie's cohorts at Rouses Point was a fellow named Thomas Barnes, aka "Bangor Billy." (Bangor is a little hamlet not so very far from Canton.) In early June 1907, Billy led a foray into the Adirondack wilds, hitting the Prime Brothers' store and post office in Upper Jay. After outfitting themselves with new clothes, shoes, hats, and neckties, plus all the groceries they could grab, the gang blew the safe and made off with about $500 in cash and checks. Billy was recognized the next day, when he was caught up in a gunfight with a posse, but he—and the rest of his party—managed to slip away into the woods.

That fall, Plattsburgh Police Chief Collins attempted a raid on the troublesome camp with a couple of railroad detectives, but word of their visit had preceded them and the place was deserted. Chief Collins must not have given up—a *Plattsburgh Sentinel* article from 1915 noted that Collins had been "instrumental" in driving those Rouses Point rascals out of the area.

Bertillon System

In the early 1880s, French anthropologist Alphonse Bertillon had a genius idea: criminals could be categorized and filed according to the measurements of their various body parts, plus hair and eye color. Along with photographs taken from the front and side views (Bertillon was the father of the mug shot), these detailed descriptions could nail repeat offenders who were trying to skate into the prison system as first timers. Bertillon also argued that the process of recording the dimensions of a suspect's individual components—from cheek and ear to foot and middle finger—made police officers more observant and effective. He was appointed Chief of the Judicial Identification Service of France in 1882.

Bertillon's idea caught on across the pond in 1887, when a warden in Illinois adopted the approach. But the system's star began to fade after little more than a decade. In the early 1900s, a widely reported case of mistaken criminal identity in Kansas underscored one of the scheme's shortcomings: two different hooligans could be similar in both measurement and appearance. The suspects' fingerprints solved the mystery, and the process of inking arrestees' digits soon superseded chronicling the breadth of their noses.

CHAPTER THREE

Safecrackers, Sneak Thieves, and Stickup Men

ROBERT BECKWITH AND CHARLES DENNEAU

"Beckwith and Denneau were described by Inspector John J. King as being fashionably dressed, and smooth talkers of excellent appearance and good manners, who frequented resorts at Bar Harbor, Me., Palm Beach, Fla., Hot Springs, Va., and the Adirondacks."

—*Lake Placid News,* August 23, 1940

To hear *Real Detective* magazine tell it, jewel thief extraordinaire Charles Denneau was caught with his pants down by Lake Placid Police Chief Francis Canfield. In the pages of an August 1941 issue of the catchpenny rag, the collar went down like this: As Chief Canfield headed for dinner at the Majestic Hotel and Restaurant one July evening in 1940, he spotted a 1936 Packard convertible coupe, license number 4C1200, whose owner had been connected to a string of gem heists. He called in reinforcements, shook down the front desk for a room number, and barged into the larcenist's lair.

As Canfield and his two backups filed in, "a young and attractive blonde, stretched out on the bed, only partly dressed, screamed." Badges were produced, clothes were hastily donned (after the platinum-haired beauty tossed a "hostile glare" at the coppers), and Denneau was taken to the station.

Titillating stuff. But a *Lake Placid News* write-up of the same event was much less lurid: Canfield spotted the car at the Majestic Restaurant, rounded up his crew, and arrested the suspect, with nary a word of a dishy dame or hot-and-heavy canoodling.

The story didn't need to be sexed up; it was already the stuff of radio melodrama. Thirty-three-year-old Denneau played the role of un-assuming magazine salesman turned jewel jacker. His partner in crime, thirty-six-year-old Robert Beckwith, was a matinee-idol wannabe who managed to score a couple of spots as an extra—including a quick cameo in Errol Flynn's swashbuckling epic *The Sea Hawk* (at least according to *Real Detective*, anyway). Together, Denneau and Beckwith infiltrated the world of the rich and famous to swipe their goodies. The pair were wildly successful, to the tune of at least $225,000 worth of baubles over a five-year period.

But there was a third actor in this drama. A Buffalo-area newspaper de-scribed Walter Miener as a "petty thief," the kind given to snatching tithes from churches or valuables from overcoats at restaurants, though he was a bit more sophisticated than that. After everything hit the fan, Miener was charged with a not-so-petty crime, the theft of $25,000 in jewels from a steamship stateroom during a fancy-pants bon voyage party at the New York docks in 1936. And he may have been the author of his own demise: *Real Detective* fingered him as the squeaky wheel that brought Denneau—and his car—to the attention of the authorities, after a disagreement over their profit-sharing plan.

Before it all fell apart, Denneau and Beckwith were living large among the beau monde. The *Long Island Daily* reported that the flimflammers "frequented swank resorts and made the acquaintance of their prospective victims beforehand so they would be sure of making successful hauls." For one caper, a $14,000 theft at the Westchester Embassy Club in 1935, Beckwith gained entrance into the ritzy country club as a guest of a fellow confidence man. During his visit, he adjourned to an upstairs retiring room and, while sauntering down the hall, snatched a jewel case from the dresser of Mrs. Joseph Politz, wife of a fabulously wealthy importer. Beckwith only got a fraction of their worth when he unloaded the spoils—$1,400 for a ring, two bracelets, and a wristwatch—but it was still a good wage for an evening's work.

Denneau and Beckwith sniffed out a few of those "swank resorts" in the fashionable Adirondacks. In August of 1937, the dapper duo schmoozed their way into the Saranac Inn, a grand hotel and cluster of waterfront cottages on Upper Saranac Lake. There they targeted Mrs. Marion Phinney, of New York City, taking the time to learn her habits as well as the layout of her cottage. She was at lunch with her personal maid in the hotel dining room, about a hundred yards from her cottage, when the pair made their precision hit. The *Plattsburgh Daily Republican* noted the

The Saranac Inn on Upper Saranac Lake attracted high-class guests—and the occasional jewel thief. COURTESY LIBRARY OF CONGRESS, LC-DIG-DET-4A06572.

professionalism of the thieves: "The gems were taken from a bureau drawer in Mrs. Phinney's bedroom without a trace of blundering or disorder." Their take that day totaled $11,000 in jewels, including a pearl necklace, diamond rings, and a pocketful of brooches and pins.

Mrs. Phinney wasn't amused. By that evening, the region's roads were crawling with state troopers. The coppers stopped cars and searched vehicles into the following morning, and sounded a three-state alarm, without so much as a stickpin to show for it. Three days later, the *Plattsburgh Daily Republican* reported that authorities thought they had the case all but solved. A Bureau of Criminal Investigation inspector had found a "definite clue" and predicted an arrest within forty-eight hours.

But the gumshoes were just blowing smoke. Denneau and Beckwith had escaped and wouldn't grace the area with their presence again until the next summer season brought a fresh round of royalty to the mountains. In July of 1938, they paid a call to Mrs. Arthur Nelson at the Lake Placid Club and walked away from her vacation cottage with a $4,500 payday. That August, Denneau made a side trip over to Essex to snatch $1,600 worth of geegaws from Mrs. T. Gilbert Pearson at the Crater Club, before heading back to the Lake Placid Club to plunder Mrs. Percy Eckhart's cabin for a $2,900 haul. (Don't feel too badly for the Lake Placid Club ladies. They belonged to an institution that admitted no members "against whom there is any reasonable social, moral, race or physical objection, or who would be unwelcome to even a small minority. . . . This invariable rule is rigidly enforced; it is found impracticable to make exceptions to Jews or others excluded, even when of unusual personal qualifications.")

The Lake Placid Club heists were kept a good deal quieter than the Phinney incident of the year before. There were no roadblocks calling attention to the robberies, nor was there any press coverage. And when Chief Canfield ran Denneau to ground in 1940, that news item was kept on the down low, too, at least at first. Authorities slapped him with a thirty-day sentence for vagrancy and hustled him to jail without fanfare. But his high life of crime was over—and it wasn't the fat lady doing the singing; it was Denneau who rolled on his partner in short order. Beckwith was captured within a month, while he was tooling around Boston in a car with Hollywood license plates. The two were charged with first-degree larceny and their old friend Walter Miener was held as a material witness. (Miener would be formally charged in September for the New York harbor heist of 1936 and shipped off to New York City for trial.)

Once they were all safely stashed in Elizabethtown's Essex County jail, the story finally hit the papers. And what a story. The local law had reeled in a couple of glamorous grifters with what the *Ticonderoga Sentinel* described as "polished manners but tarnished pasts." Denneau and Beckwith were being linked to jobs in Santa Barbara, California (Mrs. Loeb, $20,000; Lady Yule, $2,000), as well as ones in Long Island and Florida. Back in Hollywood, Beckwith had supposedly snatched $900 in jewels from the actress Merle Oberon, of *The Scarlet Pimpernel* and *Wuthering Heights* fame, and in Boston he relieved actor Leslie Howard of shiny things totaling $25,000.

In October, a grand jury indicted Denneau and Beckwith on four crimes: a $33,000 grab from Mrs. Harry Goetz, in Palm Springs, California, plus the Phinney, Eckhart, and Nelson scores. Denneau alone was nailed

For their crimes, Beckwith and Denneau both served time behind the walls of Dannemora Prison. COURTESY OF THE ADIRONDACK MUSEUM, BLUE MOUNTAIN LAKE.

for the Crater Club caper. But, in the end, the pair pleaded guilty to just one indiscretion: the Eckhart haul.

They didn't go to prison right away; the sentences of the prolific confidence men were deferred so they could lend a hand to New York City District Attorney Thomas Dewey, who was investigating a sprawling network of traffickers dealing in stolen merchandise. Denneau and Beckwith were quite accommodating—Assistant District Attorney Lawrence McKenna said they'd "received so much cooperation from the defendants" that they decided to keep them around for a few months. McKenna noted that "the probe may result in dramatic disclosures of nation-wide interest in regard to fences." But the only arrest that hit the *New York Times* was that of a sixty-year-old jeweler who paid $3,100 for a ring from one of the pair's Santa Barbara jobs.

Denneau and Beckwith kept company with Dewey and friends until January of 1941, when they were returned to Essex County to hear their fates. They didn't get much of a break for their cooperation: Denneau was sentenced to not less than three and a half years or more than seven at Dannemora's Clinton Prison and Beckwith was given four to eight at the same retreat. ⇒⊩

CHAPTER FOUR

Safecrackers, Sneak Thieves, and Stickup Men

MYSTERIOUS MONTAGUE

"One of the most daring and desperate holdups in the history of Northern New York occurred at the restaurant of Kin Hana . . . and as a result one of the bandits is dead, another is in the Essex county jail . . . officials are searching for two other men who were engaged in the thrilling affair."

—*The Adirondack Record,* August 7, 1930

O n a lonely stretch of Route 9N between Au Sable Forks and Jay, Japanese immigrant Kin Hana ran a popular roadhouse during Prohibition—a place where locals knew they could get a snort or two as needed. Since the restaurant was stationed on a busy hooch highway, Hana's cousin-in-law, bootlegger Roger Norton, thought it might be the perfect spot for a liquor drop. So in the summer of 1930, Norton and his buddies LaVerne Moore and William Carleton stopped by to scope out the scene. The gang decided it was a bad bet as a gin stash, but they saw other possibilities in a secluded joint that was often flush with cash.

Around 1:30 in the morning on August 5, 1930, as Mrs. Hana and an employee, Paul Poland, were cleaning up after a rollicking supper dance, three men with white masks barged into the restaurant.

Mrs. Hana thought it was some friends pulling a prank until she got a load of the pistols they were packing. She and Poland were ordered to the floor, along with Kin, who had just returned from the storehouse; the three were bound and gagged with torn sheets from the family's adjoining living quarters. The bandits picked Kin's pockets and emptied the cash register before one of the men marched Mrs. Hana to a backroom safe and forced her to give up the combination, threatening to break out the nitroglycerin if she didn't comply. The commotion woke up the Hanas' daughters, who were dragged out of bed and tied up with the rest.

Kin's father-in-law, Matt Cobb, wasn't so easy to subdue. Cobb was a scrapper from way back, and when one of the bandits was rude enough to jerk him awake, he decided to teach the fellow a lesson. His assailant yelped for backup and a hulking man rushed in, hit Cobb with the butt of his gun and tied him up. But Cobb wasn't quite done—the sixty-seven-year-old tore himself loose and jumped through a window. Outside he was surprised to find his cousin Norton acting as lookout, but the two didn't have time to catch up. Cobb's friend from inside flew out the door and tackled him from behind, tumbling them both down the riverbank.

The Hana Restaurant on Route 9N. COURTESY OF THE HANA FAMILY.

The outlaw barked for a blackjack and Cobb was beaten senseless.

The robbers scored about $700 and peeled off in two roadsters. But 9N was as popular with cops as it was with the bootleggers they were out to collar, and officers posted along the highway couldn't miss a car tearing toward Upper Jay at two in the morning. While they were busy chasing it down, the second vehicle slipped away.

The first car almost slipped away too. After the driver pulled a U-turn, his passenger, John Sherry, leaned over and snapped off the lights—an old rum-running trick. Except the man at the wheel, William Carleton, wasn't expecting to work blind. He missed a curve at high speed and crashed through a guard rail, flipping the car several times. The cops found Carleton near the wreckage, dazed and bloody. Sherry was dead.

They searched the vehicle for liquor and instead uncovered revolvers and a crude blackjack—a fifteen-inch length of hose weighted with buckshot—as well as golf clubs and a Gladstone bag. The tote was stuffed with the personal effects of a Mr. LaVerne Moore, including his driver's license and newspaper clippings celebrating his sporting feats. Down the road they found a pillowcase loaded with loot.

By that time Mrs. Hana had worked herself free and called the police, who were quick to make the connection to the wreck down the road. Carleton was positively identified for his part in the crime and trucked off to the Essex County lockup. And Roger Norton, who knew he had been recognized by his kin, turned himself in within days. Investigators were sure LaVerne Moore—a baseball and golf prodigy from Syracuse—was the fourth bandit, but he had already lit out of town by the time detectives knocked on his mother's door. Mary Moore swore she had no idea where he had gone.

For years, there was no sign of Moore, though detectives noted his reputation for spectacular trick shots on local golf courses and kept an eye out for up-and-coming linksmen. They got a break seven years later, when word began to trickle out of Hollywood of a camera-shy greens giant named John Montague who ran with the caviar set. It was rumored that Montague had beat his pal Bing Crosby in a one-hole match using only a baseball bat, a shovel, and a rake. (He drove with the bat, freed himself from a sand trap with the shovel, and knocked in the putt, pool-cue-style,

LaVerne Moore, aka John Montague, demonstrates one of his trademark novelty shots, chipping out of a sand trap with a spade. COURTESY CORBIS IMAGES, USED WITH PERMISSION, ALL RIGHTS RESERVED.

with the wrong end of the rake). And he was lauded—in the days before PETA—for nailing a bird off a telephone wire with a powerful drive from one of his supersized clubs. Folks said the good-natured, dimple-faced figure could lift an automobile and toss his rotund roommate, Oliver Hardy, onto a bar with one hand.

His privacy hang-ups won him titles like "the Garbo of Golf" and "the Phantom of the Fairway." No one could convince him to enter a tournament, though his skill with a club gained him some impressive fans, including top sports writer Grantland Rice. Rice was blown away, calling Montague the best golfer he'd ever seen. Unfortunately, Rice's devotion gained Montague the notoriety he was hoping to avoid.

In January of 1937, *Time* magazine broke the story of "Mysterious Montague," a links legend who shot in the 60s but panicked at the sight of press: "He could put an approach shot within ten feet of the pin from any distance up to 200 yards. He bet he could knock a ball three-quarters of a mile in five shots and won easily." The article reported that freelance photographer Bob Wallace followed Montague onto the course, hiding in the bushes to get a shot. Montague heard the shutter and stomped over. Since Montague was "built like a wrestler, with tremendous hands, bulldog shoulders and biceps half again as big as Jack Dempsey's," the photographer was quick to hand over the plate. But Wallace had been smart enough to slip the film to his brother and replace it with a blank before Montague could demand the evidence.

Once that article made the rounds—even though the picture was too poor for proper ID—the game was up. New York detectives were on to Montague, and sent a packet of LaVerne Moore's pictures, fingerprints, and writing samples to Los Angeles. Authorities there made a match and snatched Montague out of his cushy new life. In July of 1937, Essex County Sheriff Percy Egglefield was on his way to the West Coast, extradition papers in hand.

Montague's A-list friends loudly protested his detention, flooding the governor's office with telegrams of support. "John Montague is one of the finest fellows who ever lived," Oliver Hardy said.

At first, Montague was contrite, telling the press, "I got into a jam when I was a wild young kid in New York. . . . I had intended going East and clearing this thing up anyway." But, when it came down to it, he wasn't all that eager to clear things up. Montague fought extradition for more than a month before finally agreeing to escort Egglefield back to Essex County.

When the thirty-two-year-old arrived in Port Henry in late August, he was met by a mob of gawkers and big-time reporters. No longer shy, Montague smiled and mugged for pictures, but refused to say a word about the charges. The press was mostly fawning; local papers reported that the prisoner had a "pleasant moon face and a nice smile" and described his snappy ensemble in breathless detail. He was chauffeured to his new digs at the Essex County jail, in Elizabethtown, with a parade of reporters and cameramen trailing along behind.

After his golf clubs were expressed from California, Montague showed off some incredible trick shots for Henry McLemore, a United Press sports writer. McLemore was "charmed no end." (Though he was impressed in spite of himself, describing Montague as "a short, chunky guy with heavy jowls who often gives the impression of surliness.")

District Attorney Thomas McDonald remained immune to Montague's charms and vehemently opposed bail, citing the Hana robbery as "the most vicious I have ever had to do with in my 10 years as District Attorney of Essex County." He was about the only one. New York Supreme Court Justice O. Byron Brewster, as he granted bail, described Montague as a "modern Jean Valjean."

When the trial started in October people flocked to the Elizabethtown courthouse, riled up by rumors that celebrities like Bing Crosby and Clark Gable would appear. The crowd, as the press liked to point out, was disproportionately female. The *New York Times* even scored a picture of Judge Brewster's daughter and Sheriff Percy Egglefield's niece begging autographs from a smiling Montague.

The state's case against Montague was nothing to smile about. Paul Poland identified the defendant as part of the group that had stopped by Hana's not long before the robbery; he overheard them discussing its merits as a liquor drop. Matt Cobb and Mrs. Hana testified that one of their masked visitors answered to the name "Verne." Then there was the little matter of LaVerne Moore's belongings showing up in the getaway car. To remove any doubt of the defendant's guilt, the D.A. brought Roger Norton to the stand to sell his friend out as the fourth accomplice—and the muscleman who took a blackjack to Matt Cobb's face. A state trooper backed Norton up, telling the court that he questioned Moore and Norton in Schroon Lake a few hours after the crime.

But Montague and his lawyer—James Noonan, a heavy hitter who had gotten gangster Dutch Schultz off the hook in a sensational 1935 trial— took the prosecution's case apart piece by piece. Noonan badgered Matt Cobb into admitting that Montague "seems too fat" to be the man who attacked him. And when William Carleton took the stand, he called his partner Norton an outright liar. (Carleton had been sentenced to fifteen years hard labor in Dannemora for the robbery, though he only served about five; the more cooperative Norton was given just two.) Carleton swore that Moore was not there the night of the robbery, that his bag and clubs had been left in the car from an earlier trip the pair took to Rochester.

Bing Crosby and other Hollywood royalty never did make an appearance, but they sent depositions attesting to the defendant's stellar character. When Montague himself took the stand, the women in the audience "drank in every word," according to the *Syracuse Journal*. He explained that he'd been embarrassed that his things were found in a criminal's car, and that was the only reason he took off for L.A. and changed his name. He testified that he was at home in Syracuse, asleep, in the early-morning hours of August 5, 1930. Sure, he knew Carleton and Norton, but, his lawyer Noonan assured the jury, "his only interest in the men was possible liquor-running, which never materialized."

The capper came when Mary Moore swore under oath that her son was indeed tucked into his childhood bed on the night of the crime. Noonan was quick to compare her word to that of Roger Norton: "If you convict this man, you must believe a squeamish, perjuring mug against the testimony of the delightful woman who is the defendant's mother."

The jury took less than five hours to set Montague free. When the not-guilty verdict was read, the crowd went wild and a grinning Montague jumped from his seat to thank the jury. The judge shut him down with a bang of his gavel. "This is no show," he scolded. Turning to the jury, Judge Harry Owen continued, "I'm sorry to say the verdict is not in accordance with what I think you should have returned." The cheerful audience paid him no nevermind. Montague was "swept from the courtroom by the crowd," wrote the *Ticonderoga Sentinel*.

The Hanas brought a civil suit against him, but the case fizzled—just like Montague's career. Initially, the instant celebrity's prospects looked especially bright. There was talk of a million-dollar deal with Paramount Pictures, and the public couldn't seem to get enough of Mysterious Montague. At his first appearance on the greens after the acquittal— a Long Island exhibition match with Babe Ruth and Babe Didrikson that November—12,000 rubberneckers mobbed the course. The crowd became so rowdy—Montague was "halfway undressed by admirers," according to the *New York Times*—that the players were forced to cede the field after only nine holes.

The Paramount deal never happened; negotiations dried up after Hollywood censors made it clear Montague's shady past would bar him from the big screen. And, worse, the out-of-shape party boy's golf game never lived up to the hype. In 1940, a *New Yorker* "Where Are They Now" article sniffed that the "somewhat portly" Montague tanked because "he is better fitted for an easygoing country-club life, in which he can impress a small circle of friends with his special talent for trick shots, than for tournament play." In the end, even that small circle became disenchanted. Montague died alone and broke in a Los Angeles motel room in 1972, at the age of sixty-eight. ⇸

Bootlegging in the Boonies

When Prohibition became law in 1920, the Adirondack region was perfectly poised to rake in some easy money. The area offered more than fifty forested miles along the Canadian border and plenty of back roads, plus the Delaware and Hudson Railway and Lake Champlain. There were a few busy points of entry—especially on Route 22 through Mooers—but it was Route 9, twisting along the Champlain Valley, that earned the official "Rum Trail" title.

Bootlegging profits weren't limited to folks making moonshine or shuttling shipments of liquor down to Albany and New York City. Farmers cashed in on a growing demand for corn, apples, and hops, and anyone stationed along busy boozeways could rent out their garages or barns as storage depots. Those who didn't take an active part in the trade usually turned a blind eye to their neighbors shenanigans—and even helped them out in a pinch. Local telephone operators were particularly accommodating, relaying messages or warning the natives when federal agents were on the prowl.

Much of the illicit traffic stuck to the eastern edges of the Adirondacks, but some of the excitement breached the wilder interiors. Since the authorities loved to set up traps south of Keeseville—coincidentally, at the base of a mountain called Poke-O-Moonshine—bootleggers veered onto Route 9N just before that hot spot. That route took them west, racing through Au Sable Forks, Upper Jay, and Keene before rejoining Route 9 below Elizabethtown.

Mounties out of Malone—State Police Troop B, aka the Black Horse Brigade—helped the feds play cops-and-robbers throughout the area, to varying degrees of success. Although many splashy busts made the papers, Johnny Law's job was a lot like that little Dutch boy with his finger in the dam. A reporter for the *Plattsburgh Republican* took it upon himself to tally the cars flying through tiny Mooers one night in 1923. In just an hour he'd counted thirty hotrods headed south.

CHAPTER FIVE

Gangs

THE WINDFALL GANG

"The Wadsworths have long terrorized the Windfall region of Hamilton County. . . . The gang threatened to kill any one who invaded their stronghold for the purpose of arresting them."

—*New York World*, June 13, 1899

I n the spring of 1899, one young man's fancy lightly turned to thoughts of crime, and William Wadsworth was nabbed burglarizing a place near Wells, in the southern Adirondacks. Had Sheriff Perkins and his deputy, William Osborne, picked up just another scofflaw-in-the-making? Nope. They had scored the weakest link in the notorious Windfall Gang, "Hamilton County's toughest gang of robbers," according to the *Gloversville Daily Leader.*

L'il William wasn't so tough. The twenty-two-year-old didn't need much convincing to spill his clan's secrets, including who was involved in the rich haul from Hosley's general store, in Wells, the previous fall. Will tattled on his cousins, Edward McGuire, James Wadsworth, and Benjamin Wadsworth. He also rolled over on his uncle Charlie Wadsworth, reputedly the toughest of the pack, and his uncle Daniel Wadsworth, the man authorities called the brains of the enterprise. Uncle Dan, wrote the *Daily Leader*, "was the instigator and planned all the burglaries and Charles Wadsworth carried them out."

When Will was done talking, he was kind enough to lead investigators to the stashed loot. Cops found suits of clothing and other ill-gotten goods under the floorboards of an old barn in the "Windfall" section of Wells, a remote stretch of wilderness the gang called home. And there was more booty stuffed in a pipe behind a crumbling stone wall. Will explained that Uncle Charlie had broken into Hosley's by smashing a cellar window and forcing his way into the main building. After he opened the door for the rest of the crew, they stripped the market of about $500 in goods. Along with shoes, jewelry, and clothing, the plunder included a pile of ginseng, a locally foraged root that commanded sky-high prices in New York City.

For a gang that had "long terrorized" the region, the Wadsworths didn't get their names in the papers much before that 1899 roundup. Their only priors—cutting timber on state land and poaching deer—were standard Adirondack indiscretions, generally applauded by the authority-averse natives. But *The History of Hamilton County* recounts some darker pastimes, like an attempted robbery of the county treasurer on a lonely country road, a "projected misdeed" that was aborted after another wagon happened along. There was also talk around town of a pack peddler who wandered up to the ring's hideout and was never heard from again.

It was all rumor and hearsay, but once William flipped on the Hosley's heist, authorities had what they needed. Daniel and his sons, James and Benjamin, were rounded up without much trouble, though Benjamin was pretty free with his opinions of Cousin Will's loose lips. The bunch was given accommodations in Lake Pleasant's Hamilton County Jail. Next, Edward McGuire was arrested after asking for directions on Gloversville's Main Street, about thirty miles to the south of Wells. His initial protestations of innocence stopped as soon as he walked into police headquarters and saw William Osborne waiting for him. Then "the appearance of the man changed," reported the *Gloversville Daily Leader*, "and he showed visible signs of fright as he was led to his cell." Cops found more spoils from Hosley's inventory in McGuire's Gloversville pad, and Deputy Sheriff Osborne soon had another full confession.

Back at Lake Pleasant, Daniel Wadsworth was able to make his $500 bail, but the others didn't have that kind of scratch sitting around. McGuire and James Wadsworth, no doubt seeing the writing on the jailhouse wall,

The jailer and his family kept close quarters with criminals at the Hamilton County Jail around the turn of the century. COURTESY OF HAMILTON COUNTY HISTORIAN.

opted to plead guilty to burglary and testify against the rest of their brethren in exchange for shorter sentences at Dannemora's Clinton Prison. The pair were banished to that frigid fortress for one year of hard labor.

Will Wadsworth, the original canary, didn't take the same deal—seems he had a change of heart after spending some time in the slammer with his kin. Instead of cooperating with authorities, he and Cousin Ben busted out of the Lake Pleasant jail in early June.

Like other one-horse Adirondack lockups of the time, the vibe at Lake Pleasant was downright neighborly. It was more of a penal bed-and-breakfast, with the jailer and his family living onsite and prisoners held to the honor system. But the Wadsworths were a different breed. Given the freedom of the jail yard with spotty supervision, Ben and Will decided that hanging around was for chumps.

Their freedom didn't last. By the next day, a posse—"armed for business," according to the *Gloversville Daily Leader*—had sniffed Ben out in a pine forest near a relative's sawmill. They surrounded the gun-toting outlaw, who was dodging between trees, and ordered him to surrender. Ben wasn't keen to oblige, but the vigilante army closing in on him changed his mind quick enough.

Though Ben was back in bondage, there was still no sign of William, and folks began to assume the worst. The *Buffalo Evening News* picked up the colorful story and ran with the family feud angle: "William gave information to officers which led to the arrest of the gang, and Benjamin has often since threatened vengeance." Ben refused to say how he came by a gun or where his brother could be found, but word on the street was there was one less Wadsworth to worry about.

Meanwhile, authorities were still on the lookout for Charles Wadsworth, the biggest and meanest of the bunch. He had vowed he would never be taken, but Deputy Sheriff Osborne was on the case, a lawman the *Warrensburgh News* called "the most fearless man in Hamilton County."

Charlie was first spotted in Indian Lake, about forty miles to the north of Wells, though he didn't stick around town long enough for the law to catch up with him. Instead, he made for his own backyard, tangled terrain where a man could hole up for the long haul. Except some neighbors noticed Charlie's wife taking up a new hobby: rambling walks in the forest carting healthy loads of provisions. With this bit of intel, Osborne and his determined posse were able to run the fugitive down in late June.

He didn't go quietly. Uncle Charlie boasted that he wouldn't be taken alive, since there wasn't a man around "slick enough" to collar him. The *Amsterdam Evening Recorder* bought into his tough talk, writing that Charlie was "a man of gigantic stature, noted for his absolute fearlessness and his readiness to fight to the bitter end." And he lived up to his reputation. Cornered at his Windfall hidey-hole, Charlie refused to surrender, holding off his pursuers with a gun. He blew a hole in Osborne's hat before taking a shot to the arm that bled the fight right out of him. After the prisoner was patched up by a doctor in Wells, Osborne—packing a double-barrel shotgun and flanked by two armed guards—escorted him to a decidedly less lenient lockdown in Lake Pleasant.

There would be no more gallivanting about the jail yard; the inmates were all properly secured in steel cages, denied even a bit of exercise in the jail corridors. Even so, young Ben tried to break out again, using one of the iron supports from his bed to twist the lock on the cell. He mangled the lock, but the door didn't give. After that attempt, the prisoners were shackled, and still the Wadsworths made one last effort to escape. Holding back a knife from dinner, Ben and Charlie fashioned a saw and were able to work through their bonds before the turnkey discovered their gambit.

William Wadsworth turned up after about a month—and not as a corpse. He had been bouncing back and forth between the Windfall and Gloversville areas, helped along by his many relatives. After he was spotted, a posse played pickle to snag him. They also grabbed a few of his kin for aiding and abetting.

In October, Charles, William, and Benjamin were paraded into the packed courthouse in chains and under armed guard. Though the *Syracuse Evening Herald* described Charles as "six feet of iron muscular manhood," the entire bunch looked "white and worn, having been closely confined since their attempt at jailbreaking."

Edward McGuire and James Wadsworth had been shipped down from Dannemora to testify, though in the end their services weren't required. Will, Ben, and Charlie accepted the inevitable and pleaded guilty to the Hosley's robbery; Will and Ben netted two and a half years each and Uncle Charlie got four. It was sure to be an awkward ride back to prison for McGuire and Wadsworth, cuddled together with the men they were prepared to sell out.

Curious residents flocked to see the show as the gang's conveyance rolled through Gloversville on the way to catch a train. The crowds got an eyeful of strongman Charles Wadsworth bound hand and foot, flanked by his nephews Ben and Will, who were handcuffed together. Edward and James must have been relieved to get their own set of shackles to share. *The Gloversville Leader* reported that "the men . . . looked perfectly capable of doing all the acts which have been attributed to them." William Osborne stood guard, revolver at the ready.

Daniel missed out on all the fun, since Sheriff Perkins couldn't pin much of anything on the slippery kingpin. In the months before his trial in spring of 1900, authorities tried to scrape together anything they could on Daniel, including blackmailing tried-and-true stool pigeons Edward McGuire and James Wadsworth.

When Edward and James were released from Dannemora in March of 1900, their old buddy Deputy Sheriff Osborne met them at the gates with fresh warrants for their arrest. Double jeopardy? Not exactly. The pair were originally charged with both burglary and grand larceny for the Hosley's operation. But in their backroom deal with the prosecutor, they only pleaded guilty to the burglary charge, leaving grand larceny on the table. So Osborne offered them the same deal: testify against your kin or you'll get the worst of it.

Perhaps their squealing days were over, as the prosecutor had to delay Daniel's trial for months while he tried to cobble together a case. When Daniel finally got his day in court, in October of 1900, he was acquitted on scanty evidence. Though the state tried to prove that Daniel planned and profited from every misdeed his clan was ever accused of, the only link to his life in crime was a single glove found in his house. It was positively identified as part of the merchandise stolen from Hosley's store, but that was easily explained: Daniel's daughter testified that she had found it on the road and brought it home. With Daniel's acquittal, the Windfall Gang—and their hit-or-miss criminal career—disappeared from the front pages.

A few of the supporting cast did resurface through the years. In 1902, the clan's nemesis, William Osborne, was felled not by a bullet but by a friendly Lake Pleasant baseball game. He was hurt at a Fourth of July scrimmage and succumbed to his injuries about a month later, at the tender age of thirty-seven.

Edward McGuire had an encore act in 1907, when he was convicted of butchering a Mayfield farmer's steer and making off with a couple of hindquarters. Though McGuire had assured his two accomplices that "the man who squeals on this job will get shot," one of those fair-weather friends was more than happy to testify for the prosecution after his account book was found by the carcass. The second conspirator—another upstanding cousin, Stephen Wadsworth—ran for the hills when he heard the law had taken an interest in his whereabouts. McGuire was sentenced to eight months in county jail for the cattle caper.

And Charles Wadsworth's wife, who'd unwittingly led authorities to her beloved's hideout back in 1899, had another brush with fame in 1913, following the death of her second husband. Eyeing her comfortable inheritance, David Kennedy's outraged relatives claimed her first marriage hadn't been properly dissolved. But Mrs. Kennedy disavowed any relationship with the notorious Windfall Gang, maintaining she had never legally married that old Wadsworth rascal in the first place. ⟞

Lake Pleasant to Dannemora

Around the turn of the twentieth century, the atmosphere at the Lake Pleasant jailhouse was so lax that it became the stuff of legend. *The History of Hamilton County* noted that at the lockup "one could always be assured of savoury home-cooked meals, a warm room, and a soft bed." In 1904, the *New York Sun* teased that the coddled prisoners would simply be denied dessert if they misbehaved. And a joke made the rounds that the jailers warned their charges to be back in their cells at a decent hour, or they'd be locked out.

The Wadsworths surely didn't find Dannemora's Clinton Prison as agreeable. The new neighborhood was bad enough—"Little Siberia," as it was known, had been plunked down in the middle of a freezing northern Adirondack nowhere. And the spot hadn't been selected solely for its depressing isolation. It was also situated alongside a handy iron-ore vein, so that inmates would have plenty of opportunity to work off their debts to society.

The first set of Dannemora-bound prisoners had arrived in Plattsburgh in the spring of 1845 and were marched seventeen hilly miles to their new home. Or, to what would become their new home, after they built it themselves. The resulting complex, surrounded by a stockade fence, could initially house 500 reprobates. (Nowadays, around 3,500 prisoners lodge behind the forty-foot-high concrete wall running down the town's main drag.)

By the time the Wadsworths arrived, the iron mining scheme—which proved unprofitable and unwieldy—had been abandoned, but there was still plenty to keep idle hands from becoming the devil's workshop. Inmates were tasked with road work and construction projects, or with pumping out shirts, sheets, and other household goods in the prison's sweatshops. And forget about washing that sweat off; jailbirds were granted only one bath every two weeks. Bellyaching or other misbehavior might bring on a beating with a leather paddle or solitary confinement in a dark room. But even that was preferable to the punishment awaiting those who'd been sentenced to the place's electric chair, which wouldn't serve its last customer until 1913.

CHAPTER SIX

Gangs

THE BLACK HAND

"The Black Hand is an organization of the most desperate gang of cut throats unhung."

— *Essex County Republican*, August 23, 1907

One May day in 1906, an Italian immigrant known as "Little Willo" was walking the tracks. He wasn't just wandering idly; as a trackwalker for the Delaware & Hudson Railway, he was responsible for inspecting the rails between Saranac Lake and Ray Brook. Along the way, Willo was accosted by three roughnecks who pummeled him and scampered away with $45 and a silver watch. He was found unconscious by the crew of a passing train and bundled off to Saranac Lake for treatment.

Later that evening, about thirty miles to the north, Navzorano Foschi and Valonfino Moroni were cooking up dinner in a Loon Lake cabin when a couple of their countrymen came a-calling. The nattily dressed travelers asked for directions to Malone, but they weren't really interested in the roommates' answer. "Without any further conversation," the *Ticonderoga Sentinel* reported, "the strangers slashed their faces with razors, laying open their cheeks." Foschi and Moroni "had previously refused to pay tribute to the 'Black Hand' organization," the article explained.

The Black Hand was one of the press's favorite boogiemen at the dawn of the twentieth century, when groups operating under that name—

or tagged with it in sensationalized newspaper reports—were popping up in big cities as well as little melting-pot company towns. The primarily Italian gangs specialized in extortion, organizing pay-to-play schemes to gouge newcomers or shaking down more prosperous citizens with letters signed by a black hand or other ominous symbols.

In New York City and Chicago, Black Hand outfits played hardball with kidnappings and explosions. Hair-raising headlines from the *New York Times*—"Black Hand Threat Fulfilled with Bomb"—and the *Chicago Tribune*—"Death by Dagger; Black Hand Acts"—scared the pants off the public. The Adirondack region had its share of splashy front-page items, like threats sent to Whitehall businessman Edgar Lowenstein in the spring of 1907. Lowenstein, a partner in the Champlain Silk Company, had been receiving a steady stream of notes demanding $3,000 in exchange for his life and the lives of his two sons. The letters, with postmarks from both New Jersey and Whitehall, were signed "Black Hand" and sported skull-and-crossbones flourishes. Lowenstein didn't fork over; instead, he surrounded his family with bodyguards and set detectives on the terrorists' trail. The promised murder and mayhem never occurred.

Black Hand plots weren't the work of a sprawling, Mafia-like clan. Far from the image of smooth Dons making offers people couldn't refuse, blackhanders were disparate packs of delinquents cashing in on the infamous name and preying on the vulnerability of immigrant communities. Breathless newspaper accounts helped sow fear and encourage cooperation, though it's difficult to tease out fact from fiction in the coverage, since the folks shilling dailies weren't always concerned with the distinction. Rumor was often enough—in 1908, when it was whispered that a former Lake Placid man had been kidnapped and killed by the Black Hand in New York City, the *Ticonderoga Sentinel* ran with the story. And a healthy dose of xenophobia was woven into regional coverage; the *Essex County Republican*, for one, was quick to throw around words like "dago."

In 1906, a criminal band dubbed the Black Hand in the local press was operating along the Delaware & Hudson's Chateaugay Railroad, which ran from Plattsburgh to Lake Placid, by way of Dannemora, Lyon Mountain, and Loon Lake. According to the *Plattsburgh Daily Press*, the scam went like this: A few days before payday, thugs would swing by and demand up to five bucks from each Italian worker. If a man failed to cough up the cash, he would be "waylaid and probably cut with a razor or pounded into unconsciousness." The article added, "Laborers are living in terror . . . even the foremen are ready to throw up their jobs and leave the country."

This atmosphere of intimidation would never do, not with captains of industry poised to lose a cheap source of labor. After Little Willo's run-in, the Plattsburgh-based detective for the Delaware & Hudson Railway, William Libby, headed down the tracks to settle the matter. In Lake Placid, Libby teamed up with a veteran officer and a posse of eager tenderfoots. They followed a lead to the hangout of a shady crew of Italian sewer workers about a mile and a half outside the village.

The posse surrounded the place, with orders to open fire on any man attempting to escape. Meanwhile, Libby and his partner burst through the shack's door, surprising three occupants. One was pretty quick on the draw—just not quick enough. The officer was able to jerk the perp's weapon away and slap him into handcuffs before he could do any damage. Another hoodlum made for a double-barreled shotgun standing in the corner, but he was soon sporting the same metal bracelets as his friend. Unfortunately, the greenhorns standing guard outside heard the scuffle and ran to give aid, allowing a third suspect to jump out a back window and disappear into the trees.

The *Plattsburgh Daily Press* speculated that the fugitive was headed toward Utica, and Libby must have agreed, since he spent a long night at Lake Clear Junction keeping an eye on all southbound trains. The two culprits who were captured were positively identified as the men who'd attacked the trackwalker. They were sent to the Essex County jail in Elizabethtown, but that didn't mean they'd do any real time.

Before the case could come before a judge, Little Willo was hunted down by henchmen and offered his cash back if he made himself scarce. He didn't bite. On the next visit, he was offered double his money. Still, he stood his ground. But that's where the negotiations stopped; in the end, Willo was informed that if he testified he'd be killed. And an article that ran in several newspapers, outlining the trackwalker's new places of employment and residence, couldn't have done much for his sense of

In the early 1900s, Jerry Blanch, aka Jerry Brancati, was the padrone, or boss, of the Lyon Mountain branch of the Black Hand. He recruited workers for the local mine, and took a cut of all financial transactions. Anyone who didn't cooperate was beaten, slashed with a knife, or made to disappear. COURTESY LAWRENCE P. GOOLEY AND JILL C. JONES OF BLOATED TOE PUBLISHING.

security. So Willo disappeared—either of his own accord or helped along by others—and his assailants were released.

The razor-wielding felons who jumped Foschi and Moroni in Loon Lake were never found, though papers reported that the duo took off in the direction of Lyon Mountain. That community, in the northernmost reaches of the Adirondack region, was a mining hub bursting with immigrants in the early 1900s and slapdash in crime control. The gossip was that the 300 or so Italian residents had their own rule of law, headed by a padrone who was paid off anytime a newbie wanted a place on the payroll. In Larry Gooley's *Lyon Mountain: Tragedy of a Mining Town*, long-time resident Oliver Pivetta explained that if an Italian needed a job, he had to ante up. "If you didn't pay," he said, "you'd take the cut. They'd use knives on you."

The Lyon Mountain rumor mill attributed these shenanigans to a local branch of the Black Hand, with Jerry Blanch, né Brancati, at its head. He fell under the eye of law enforcement only a couple of times: once, in 1906, when a constable was shot in the back on election night, and again in 1909, after a pair of his lackeys were tried for selling liquor without a license following a shooting and slashing incident at Blanch's boarding house. (In the latter case, the *Plattsburgh Daily Press* wrote that one of the witnesses bore a "shocking scar from the very edge of the eye socket down the cheek and up the other side.") Blanch was never convicted of any wrong-doing—that honor was reserved for the gang over at Mineville, in the Champlain Valley.

In the summer of 1907, the bosses at Witherbee-Sherman Mining Company, headquartered in Port Henry, heard that a Black Hand group from Albany was headed to their works at Mineville. It wasn't long before the company detective, former Plattsburgh police chief William Fitzgerald, began hearing that workers were being threatened for cash, though nobody was willing to talk on the record. Even so, the *Essex County Republican* reported, "Fitzgerald was satisfied that there was an organized branch of the Black Hand at work in Mineville."

The detective got a break in the case when the gang decided to pick on Michael Morrazzo, a clerk for the Witherbee-Sherman Company. Morrazzo received a letter demanding $30 in August; when he ignored it, he was taken up and beaten. After his licking, he was told to bring $40 to a house on Mineville's Barton Hill the following Sunday—otherwise he'd be killed. So Morrazzo began begging around town for a loan to pay off the thugs. Once Fitzgerald heard the news, he hatched an easy sting operation: Morrazzo was given a wad of marked bills and sent up Barton Hill. Fitzgerald followed, backed up by eighteen armed men.

After Morrazzo made the transaction, the posse stormed the building, rifles raised. Four blackhanders gave themselves up right off; three more escaped in a barrage of bullets, though two of them were scooped up soon after. Inside the house, Fitzgerald found a list of the group's members along with the marked bills. He'd also scored the leader of the bunch, twenty-six-year-old Joseph Fransica. (Or Francica or Francico or Fransico. Trying to nail down the correct spelling of a foreign name in the turn-of-the-century North Country? Fuggetaboutit.) Fransica and his flunkies were shipped to the Port Henry jail and held on $3,000 bail each. The next day, according to the *Ticonderoga Sentinel*, two dozen Italians flooded out of town.

Two more members of the outfit were arrested the following month, accused of robbing a fellow miner of $150. The victim had been getting notes demanding money for some time, so he decided America wasn't for him and took off for the homeland. But he didn't make it far. The pair of ruffians intercepted him at the train station in Crown Point and dragged him back to Mineville, where he was forced to hand his savings over to Fransica. The kidnappers were identified and arrested as they stepped off a pit car after their shift at the mines.

The Elizabethtown courthouse was packed for the December trials, thanks to the bumper crop of witnesses who finally agreed to go on record, with a lot of help from interpreters. After the court plodded through ten days of testimony, Fransica was convicted of robbery and extortion; he was sentenced to nine and a half years in Dannemora's Clinton Prison. (The extortion charge stemmed from a $100 fleecing of one of Fransica's frightened pen pals.) Once the leader went down, three of his henchmen opted to plead guilty. Frank Augastina and Frank Corbo each got a year in Dannemora; eighteen-year-old Gerolomo Utta was slapped with an open-ended sentence at Elmira Reformatory. A fourth, Antonio Simona, took his chances at trial and came away with two years in the big house for ex-tortion. The *Ticonderoga Sentinel* called the convictions "the first obtained in the state for Black Hand work." Three other gang members traded their testimony for get-out-of-jail-free cards.

Fransica was clamoring to get out of Dannemora by 1915, arguing that he was a goner anyhow, thanks to a case of consumption. Consumption or not, the kingpin wouldn't breathe free again until June of 1917. News of his release made plenty of people near his old home base nervous, especially the witnesses for the prosecution. But Fransica returned to

Mineville just long enough to hear that authorities were on the lookout for him before taking off for a friendlier neighborhood.

By the time that Fransica was back on the streets, the Black Hand's star was fading anyway. Some of the last regional ink wasted on the gangs was hearsay printed in the *Ticonderoga Sentinel* that a 1925 knife and gun fight amongst Italians in a Fort Edward restaurant involved members of a Black Hand operation working Washington County. But the real money had moved on to bootlegging, a racket capturing the imagination of most up-and-coming criminals—and the attention of the press. ⇥

Origins of the "Black Hand"

In the popular imagination, the Black Hand and the Mafia were two branches of the same nefarious family tree, kissing-cousin criminal enterprises that flourished in Italy and crossed the Atlantic with boatloads of immigrants. But that's not really the way of it, according to Gaetano D'Amato, former President of the United Italian Societies, who did some myth-busting in a 1908 *North American Review* article. The Black Hand—a name borrowed from Spanish, not Italian, anarchists—was born and bred in the United States, as American as swiping your neighbor's apple pie. The phenomenon germinated around the turn of the century, after a couple of splashy crimes committed under the "Black Hand" flag gave the name a headline-grabbing mystique. Its use snowballed from there, as far-flung criminal elements—and enterprising editors—dogpiled on the buzzword's sinister reputation.

The Adirondacks of the early twentieth century, where mining, logging, and railroad companies were busily exploiting work-starved foreigners, was fertile ground for Black Hand operations. Immigrant tribes often remained insulated, cut off from their wider communities by language, by culture, by suspicion. In company-controlled enclaves, law enforcement was spotty and arbitrary—like everything else, at the pleasure of the company. But black-handers didn't have a monopoly on felonious behavior. And, really, for intimidation and exploitation on a massive scale, nobody could beat the companies themselves.

Manhunts

CHARLES PARKER

*"The feeling among the guides and others in the region
where [Charles Parker] committed the outrage is very
intense against him, and if those hardy and bold fellows
should take the law into their own hands, short work
would be made of the brute."*

—*Lowville Journal and Republican*, August 4, 1881

During the second half of the nineteenth century—the heyday of the
Adirondack guide—those quirky backwoods characters were a leg-
endary breed. But in the late summer of 1881, one of their number
hit the front pages under banners like "miscreant" and "villain." And some
of that negative ink splashed over to others in the trade.

Adirondack guides were being slandered to such a degree that
George Washington Sears, aka Nessmuk, whose glowing letters from
the North Woods helped popularize outdoor adventuring, felt the need
to defend the group's honor. In an issue of *Forest and Stream* that year,
he wrote, "A guide's religion is, first and foremost, to take care of his
'party'—to defend, protect, feed, shelter and bring through safely . . .
at the risk of his life, if need be."

The whole kerfuffle started when Mrs. George Bull, wife of the
chairman of the Democratic Committee in Philadelphia, took a trip to

the Long Lake camp of her brother-in-law, Connecticut Senator Oliver Platt. Bull, a "strong, plucky little woman of very attractive appearance," according to the *Albany Evening Times*, took the usual route into the North Country, riding the Adirondack railroad to North Creek and hopping the stage to Blue Mountain Lake. She was traveling solo—her husband would follow later—but her travels weren't lonely for long. By happy coincidence, Mrs. Bull made the acquaintance of Mr. and Mrs. Hall when the coach stopped at the North River Hotel for lunch.

Since the Halls were also headed to Platt's spread, the crew took off together to Blue Mountain Lake. Only Mrs. Bull's trunk didn't make the stage. Mr. and Mrs. Hall gamely offered to wait it out with their new friend, but their patience had limits. When the wayward trunk still hadn't arrived the next day, the Halls set off without its owner, who assured them she would follow along soon enough.

Once the trunk caught up with her, Mrs. Bull found herself alone in the Adirondacks, and in need of a guide. The job went to Charles Parker, a middle-aged transplant to the area who made his living filling hotel tables with fresh fish and wild game. (He was rumored to be an ex-con shacking up with his third wife, and not bothering with the formality of a divorce from the other two.) The regular guides must have all been hired out, since Parker took over those duties only when there was no one else available. The *Albany Evening Journal* reported that he was "pointed out as a safe and reliable man," though they neglected to say who did the pointing. And with this dubious introduction, the pair started their eighteen-mile backcountry journey.

They left from Miron Fletcher's Forked Lake House on July 23, paddling north on the 1,200-acre Forked Lake and into the Raquette River. They crossed two carries without incident (stretches where adventurers had to disembark and tramp through the woods, carrying the boat rather than vice versa). But when Parker and Mrs. Bull reached the final carry, a hike around Buttermilk Falls, the peaceful Adirondack backdrop showed its true nature—a wild frontier where the strong could make their own rules. What happened in that lonely spot must be left to the imagination, shaped only by nineteenth-century euphemisms: a "fiendish" and "brutal outrage," an "indecent assault on the person of Mrs. George Bull."

The *Watertown Re-Union* wrote that Parker "almost strangled her and tore her clothing into shreds." Only a couple of papers dared call the deed what it was: attempted rape.

The *Albany Evening Journal* reported that, after the attack, Parker "extorted a promise of silence from the lady under threats of drowning." And he must have been reasonably sure of Mrs. Bull's compliance, since he blithely ferried her right to Platt's doorstep. Mr. Hall would later tell a reporter that he knew immediately that something was wrong when he met the boat at the shore. Perhaps it was the "attack of hysteria" that the *Evening Journal* attributed to Mrs. Bull.

With the lady fainting away and reinforcements rushing in, Parker tried to push off from shore, but Mr. Hall caught his boat by the bow. Deciding he didn't want to see the end of this show, Parker jumped ashore and made off into the woods. After a quick stop back at his Forked Lake cabin, to grab his rifle—and perhaps to let his wife know he would be more than a little late for dinner—he beat feet for Canada.

Meanwhile, telegrams describing Parker and his crime raced around the region. Led by Constable Warren Cole, of Long Lake, a posse took off in pursuit of the culprit. But, in the deep recesses of the Adirondacks, it wasn't easy to find a man who didn't want to be found. Especially one familiar with the lay of the land. The quarry made it to Lowville, about fifty miles to the west as the crow flies, and traded in his gun for a new suit of clothes and a little pocket money. Then he hopped a train to Watertown. From there, it was just a quick trip over the border.

On July 28, Parker wandered into a Kingston, Ontario, police station and as good as turned himself in. Using the name George Wright, he asked the officers if he needed a permit to drum up business for his trade, silver plating. Since word of Parker's offense had preceded him, along with a detailed description of the suspect, the cops' reply was the slam of a jail cell door.

The *Watertown Re-Union* explained that his cover was blown by the fresh scar on his nose and a missing finger. Parker's jailers had also noticed that his mustache had been hastily dyed black. But, despite his uncanny similarities to the wanted man, the prisoner stuck to his story, calmly spinning out the details of George Wright's life and his most recent whereabouts. That Parker fellow investigators kept going on about? He'd never heard of him.

The tough cookie began to crumble only after investigators found a receipt made out to Chas. Parker in George Wright's personal effects.

Watertown officials soon arrived to wrangle Parker back over the border, where he finally copped to his real name. He had a good sit-down with a friendly ear, telling a reporter his tale of woe. He lived in Forked Lake, he explained, with his wife of about a year, making ends meet by hunting and fishing for the Blue Mountain House. He was engaged as a guide to Mrs. Bull, sure, but the pair had had a fine time on their foray through the wilderness. They both had brought along whiskey, and neither were shy about drinking it. When he dropped his new friend off at Platt's, he was surprised to overhear Mrs. Bull tell one of the party that he had "insulted her" on the journey. He didn't stick around to hear the rest.

The *Re-Union* gave "no credence" to the consensual bacchanal story—and neither did Constable Cole. When he arrived on the scene, after a thirty-hour nonstop trip by stage and train, Parker was dragged back to the central Adirondacks to answer for the assault. (As they travelled through Lowville, Parker was heckled at the depot—or, as the *Lewis County Democrat* put it, "he was treated with some pretty free expressions of opinion upon his outrageous crime.") Cole was taking no chances with his slippery charge; he handcuffed Parker to his own wrist to keep him from running off again. But Parker just bided his time.

How he escaped is a bit of a puzzler. The *Albany Argus* wrote that Parker's handcuffs were removed once the party arrived in the Long Lake area and the prisoner, spotting an opportunity, raced back off into the woods. But the *Watertown Re-Union* and several other outlets reported that Cole and Parker were shackled together when they went to bed on August 2, and that Cole woke up alone. No one could say how Parker loosed his bonds, though the press found a more absorbing mystery in his choice of clothing. Parker's slacks were still hanging at the hotel; Cole's garments were similarly unmolested. "The only question is," pondered the *Re-Union*, "whose pants did Parker wear in his last flight?" Indeed.

The constable was forced to start the hunt without that vital piece of wardrobe information. And his cause was further hampered by the fact that Parker was in his old stomping grounds, with his wife and friends on hand to help him survive in the backwoods. Still, it ended badly for

Warren Cole, of Long Lake, didn't get famous for shooting a desperado in the backcountry—instead, he's remembered as a master boat builder and respected Adirondack guide. COURTESY OF THE ADIRONDACK MUSEUM, BLUE MOUNTAIN LAKE.

Parker, back where it all started, on the shores of Forked Lake.

The *Glens Falls Times* implied that a meeting had somehow been brokered between the pursuers and their prey on the morning of August 5, and that Constable Cole had shattered the truce with gunfire. But at the coroner's inquest into the affair that would follow in September, William Kelley, who was tagging along during the search, offered a different version of events.

Kelley testified that he and Cole took a lunch break by the lake that day on the north side of Forked Lake. Wandering around after he ate, Kelley heard voices coming from the cabin of William Cross. Suspecting that Parker was eating dinner there, he ran back to tell Cole. The constable took off to investigate, while Kelley, somewhat inexplicably, chose that exciting moment in the chase to lie down and take a nap. He was roused by voices: Cole was hollering to Parker, who was in a boat, to come ashore and turn himself in; Parker was replying in the negative. Kelley heard Cole repeat his order three times, then heard a gunshot, which finally caused the snoozer to bestir himself and run down to the lake. Once there, he heard Parker say, "Warren, you have shot me," and saw him fall back into his boat.

So Kelley, belatedly acting the hero, swam out and commandeered the boat. He picked up the constable and rowed the wounded fugitive back to William Cross's cabin. Though a doctor who was vacationing in Raquette Lake was brought in, Parker succumbed to his wounds.

The inquest included testimony from a Mr. Orrin Lapell, who had lunched with the wanted man at Cross's cabin that day. Lapell corroborated Kelley's version of events, adding that Parker had boasted during the meal that "he had a friend that would not back for an officer"—Parker's "friend," Lapell explained, was his gun. When William Cross took the stand, he testified that Parker had a gun in his hand when he came to the cabin and he kept the weapon at the ready while he ate. But Cross also said that, after the showdown, he heard Parker cry, "Mr. Cole, you have shot an innocent man."

The coroner's jury disagreed. Considering Parker was on the run from a violent crime, and since an old single-barreled breech-loader rifle was found in the bottom of his boat, Parker was deemed "armed and desperate." The panel ruled that Warren Cole had shot him "while in the discharge of his duty as a constable."

Though the *Glens Falls Times* indicated that Cole was a persona non grata in the area following the affair, and that the brotherhood of Adirondack guides would seek vengeance for the death of one of their own, Nessmuk told a different tale in *Field and Stream*. Parker was "not a guide, and never pretended to be one," Nessmuk explained. "The guides say that Parker was an assumed name—that he was a convict who had served a term in the penitentiary." And they were happy to see the last of him.

As for Cole, he became a respected member of the Adirondack Guides' Association, a union that was organized a decade later. In 1898, he represented Long Lake at the association's Adirondack display for the Sportsmen's Exhibition in Madison Square Garden, showing off one of his beautifully crafted guideboats. (The *New York Mail and Express* was more impressed with the guides themselves, calling the Adirondack contingent "magnificent specimens of physical manhood.") ⇥

Adirondack Guides

When tourists tripped into the Adirondacks, they needed someone to show them a good time. And that someone was an Adirondack guide, a woods-savvy servant who may not have recently washed behind his ears, but who could lead sportsmen and women (known as "sports") to the richest hunting grounds and the sweetest fishing spots. On the trail, the guide was responsible for carting the gear, cooking the grub, cobbling together a shelter from the bounty of the forest, and entertaining the city slickers with tales of adventure. To transport paying customers around the backcountry, guides favored small wooden vessels—double-ended rowboats—that could be easily carried around rapids or from one pond the next.

Not all guides were created equal: all it took to be a guide was to say you were one. In his 1869 *Adventures in the Wilderness*, William H. H. Murray lauded hardworking self-employed guides as "bronzed and hardy, fearless of danger, eager to please," while dismissing some inexperienced specimens hired by hotels as "inferior, and given to drunkenness."

There were guiding superstars, like John Cheney (1800-1887), who guided the first recorded ascent of New York's tallest peak, Mount Marcy, and claimed to have gone head-to-head with both panther and wolf. But for his money, mid-nineteenth-century author B. J. Lossing favored Abnaki guide Mitchell Sabattis (possibly 1824-1906), calling the Long Laker "by far the best man in all that region to lead the traveler to . . . the Adirondack mountains."

The quirky woodsman poet from Keene Valley, Orson "Old Mountain" Phelps (1816-1905), was memorialized—and catapulted to fame—by an 1878 *Atlantic Monthly* essay calling him "the discoverer of the beauties and sublimities of the mountains." Alvah Dunning (1816-1902) had a reputation of being a bit more ornery—but as the only year-round resident of Raquette Lake for years, I suppose he had that right. About his customers, he is said to have griped, "They pay me well enough, but I'd rather they stayed out of my woods. . . . They're mostly darned fools, anyhow."

CHAPTER EIGHT

Manhunts

+===========+

ALVIN "SAM" PASCO

*Alvin "Sam" Pasco's "vicious and revengeful nature and
lawless acts have for thirty years made his name a terror
in his native town of Thurman."*

—*Warrensburgh News*, April 25, 1918

Charles Pasco was a chicken thief, shot dead robbing Squire Barber's henhouse in the 1870s. And he was a choirboy compared to some of the others in his Thurman-based clan. His brother, Leander Pasco, was so querulous that local lore says his relatives drew lots for the privilege of gunning him down. The honors went to Joseph "Cal" Wood, who had joined the loving family when he married Leander's daughter Mattie. At Cal's trial, a neighbor testified that Mattie smiled when she heard word of her father's death. Her smile didn't last; Cal was the first man to take a ride in Dannemora's electric chair, on August 2, 1892.

But the award for outstanding outlaw in the Pasco tribe has to go to Leander's son Alvin "Sam" Pasco, a six-and-a-half-foot giant of a man. He ran wild after his father was killed in 1890, when Sam was in his teens. (Sam's mama had died just a year before.) The *Troy Times* wrote that Sam "helped himself to the property of other people whenever he wanted it, and met protests with his fists or threats to shoot." And the *Glens Falls Morning Star* dubbed him the "Thurman Terror." Even so, the law didn't trouble him much until 1898, when he scored a six-month stint in an Albany pen for assault. The charge stemmed from an incident that October, when Sam put a bullet in the thigh of the Thurman constable, Charles "Tuck" Wood, while the lawman was attempting to arrest him for stealing some sheep. Sam's excuse was that he mistook Tuck (who was Cal Wood's brother) for Henry Mosher, another acquaintance he was currently feuding with.

Sam hit the big time in 1903, when a grand jury indicted him for lighting a string of forest fires, as well as on charges of assault and burglary. The sheriff was dispatched to bring him in, but someone tipped Sam off that the law was coming and he "deserted his old haunts with suspicious haste," according to the *Morning Star*. He was finally tracked down at a cohort's home in Stony Creek and dragged back to be tried.

The *Warrensburgh News* reported that Pasco pleaded guilty to "willfully setting fire to standing timber," but he didn't take any of it very well, especially not his indeterminate sentence of up to four years in Dannemora. (The warden at Clinton Prison predicted that he would serve the full four.) In 1906, the district attorney who tried the case, William Kiley, heard from a recent parolee that Sam was bragging that he'd get even with Kiley and the supervisor of Thurman once he was free. That big talk backfired; when Sam was released, in July of 1907, Kiley—now a judge—gave him a return ticket to jail on the 1903 burglary charge.

All that time in prison didn't improve Sam's social skills. Back in Thurman in 1910, he was ambushed by an admirer near Ransom Wilsey's place, taking a gunshot to the hip that laid him out in the road. When Sam regained his feet, he spotted Wilsey walking toward his barn with what looked like a gun (although he later admitted to authorities it could have been a crowbar). That was enough for Sam, who was sure the well-respected sixty-three-year-old farmer was the one who did him dirty. En route to the Glens Falls hospital, Sam stopped by Warrensburg to file a complaint with the justice. Wilsey was arrested, but swore he didn't do it, saying he had no trouble with Pasco. Besides, he hadn't even fired a gun in decades. Justice Hodgson was convinced, and the matter was dropped. The identity of the ill-wisher who pulled the trigger would remain a mystery—except to Sam, who stuck by his original theory and ranted that old

Wilsey would pay for his misdeed. Wilsey died more than a dozen years later of natural causes, though some gossips claimed his health was poor because he'd spent almost a decade living in fear of Pasco.

Sam's next dustup made the *Warrensburgh News* in 1912, when one of his buddies broke into his home and stole a prime coon skin—"which Sam had carefully selected from his season's catch for the express purpose of providing himself with a piece of headgear for the next winter." The robber also got away with a mileage book, but it was the loss of that fine fur that made Sam mad enough to switch allegiances: the perennial bad-boy was suddenly a friend to law and order, insisting that his former pal be arrested and prosecuted to the fullest extent.

That same year he was busted for taking timber off another neighbor's property (harvesting other people's trees was rumored to be one of his favorite pastimes). The judge slapped him with a ten-year sentence, then offered Sam a way out. All would be forgiven, he decreed, if the defendant would just make himself scarce. Sam had ten days to wrap up any local business and leave the county; he showed his gratitude by parading around town with a shotgun after the deadline had passed. When he finally moseyed on down to the Glens Falls area, it was too late—the deal was off the table. Authorities tracked Sam down and gifted him with a decade in Dannemora.

That was a sentence Sam had no intention of finishing. Within a year he tried to escape—in a body bag—by swallowing crushed glass and, when that didn't work, refusing to eat. But he managed to survive long enough to see his sentence downsized to five years, thanks to an eager young Saranac Lake lawyer, Francis Cantwell, who took an interest in the case. Cantwell managed to convince the governor that Sam's punishment was overly harsh for a little bit of lumber larceny.

When Sam was released at the beginning of 1918, he settled into a lumbering job near Glens Falls and kept his nose clean for a bit. But he knew that his cousin and her husband, Orlie Eldridge, had moved into his Thurman homestead—the couple claimed half-ownership in the spread— and that just didn't sit well with Sam. So, in early April, he traveled back to town to sort the matter out. His first order of business was a call at the Warrensburg newspaper office, where he placed an ad outlining his zero-tolerance policy for trespassers on his Thurman property. Then he paid a visit to his old friend James Maxim, who lived near the disputed property, and secured himself a Winchester rifle.

Gun in hand, Sam headed to his old residence, where he explained to the family of nine that it would be in their best interests to leave. After some discussion he'd softened his stance enough to allow the women and children to remain, though Orlie was a different matter. Sam forced the farmer out at the point of his gun, and Eldridge went, sure enough—straight to the deputy sheriff. Sam Pasco wasn't an individual the deputy wanted to take on alone, so he sent for the state troopers, who had been newly stationed over in Warrensburg. (The New York State Troopers, a mounted force charged with protecting the rural pockets of the state, was created only a year before.)

Troopers Herrick and Kelly arrived at Maxim's cabin the next morning and found Sam inside, holding tight to his borrowed rifle. They managed to talk Sam into having a discussion with Eldridge, but couldn't convince him to leave the gun behind. He said he needed to bring it along so he could give it back to its rightful owner, which sounded reasonable enough. But letting Sam Pasco keep his gun was a rookie mistake. Outside, they met up with Orlie and started to parley. As the group walked toward the Eldridge place, it looked like Sam and Orlie might come to a neighborly resolution. Instead, Sam ended the argument with a bullet to his cousin-in-law's gut. The fatally wounded man fell into Trooper Kelly's arms, and Sam swung on Herrick, putting a bullet hole in the trooper's coat but leaving his skin intact.

Pasco knew when to fold 'em—he raced toward a wooded swamp, dodging some answering fire. Then he zigged when he should have zagged and took some lead himself, though he was still able to limp into the wilderness. And so the manhunt was on, a first for the freshly minted troopers. Kelly and Herrick called in reinforcements from their barracks, and borrowed some bloodhounds from a nearby prison. Wanted posters were slapped up around the region, offering $500 cash to anyone who could bring in Pasco, dead or alive. *The Grey Riders*—a schmaltzy version of the state troopers' early adventures that hit bookshelves in 1922—described the image that appeared on the placard: "Hair, matted and coarse as a straw hatch, grows down low over the narrow forehead. The eyes, sunk beneath overhanging brows, have the bleak, insolent stare of a hawk. The cheeks are thick, the jaw heavy, and the mouth is a straight, cruel slash across the lower face."

The deck was stacked against the lawmen from the start. Sam wouldn't be easy to find on his home turf, especially not after a rainstorm obliterated his scent. He knew the territory, he was a good shot, and he was desperate. The *Warrensburgh News* predicted that Pasco would "resist capture to the last and sell his life as dearly as possible." The troopers couldn't count on much help from the locals, either. Sam had a lot of friends in the area—and even if some of his neighbors didn't care for him very much, they liked the troopers even less, the newest pack of outsiders pushing into the territory to boss around the natives.

But after being skunked for ten days, the lawmen got the lead they were looking for: Sam had been hanging out in a friend's farmhouse up in "the Glen." A few accounts speculate that they got the tip from the home's owner, Enock Hewitt, who was rather put out by his unexpected guest. Others insist Hewitt remained true to his old friend, and that it was a neighbor, or perhaps Hewitt's wife, who alerted authorities to Pasco's presence. Either way, the Warren County sheriff and half a dozen troopers were on the case, surrounding the cottage and waiting for their quarry to appear. That happened around 11 p.m., when Sam went out for some air after a quiet dinner. Hewitt followed him to the door with his lantern; some say it was so the men outside would have a clear shot. As Sam stepped out the door—his trusty rifle well out of reach—a bullet breezed by him. He turned to run back inside, but was cut down where he stood. "Don't shoot again," Sam pleaded, "I'm done for all right."

The troopers trucked in a doctor from Warrensburg to patch the prisoner up, and the doc agreed with Sam's initial assessment—the Warren County wild man was a goner for sure. But Sam managed to last through the night and, though his breathing became labored, he talked freely with his executioners. He explained that he had no choice in the Eldridge matter: he was sure Eldridge was bent on killing him, so he took him out first. After the murder, Sam said he lived poorly, hiding in a cave where he could start a fire without being seen and heading to civilization only when he was desperate for something to eat. He described his suffering

Alvin "Sam" Pasco is buried in the Pasco family cemetery in Warren County, New York. PHOTOGRAPH BY NIKI KOUROFSKY.

from the cold and from the wound Trooper Herrick had doled out as he was running for the hills. Sam claimed he had already made up his mind to surrender. "It looked as though they were sure to get me anyway," he admitted, "and I was tired of it all."

Sam Pasco's body was carted to a Warrensburg undertaker, where hundreds of people flocked to get a look at the famous felon—the local school even cancelled classes on the day of his funeral so everyone could attend. He was buried in a small cemetery just north of Thurman, in a coffin that had to be special ordered to fit his sprawling frame. Some retellings of the Sam Pasco saga say he's buried under a giant boulder or resting just outside the cemetery's gates, banished from his family's plot because of his crimes. But he's there in the Pasco Cemetery, lying under a tiny stone—an unimpressive bit of reality sitting in the shadow of his massive legend. ⇥

Cal Wood's Execution at Dannemora

From the *Albany Argus*, 3 August, 1892:

In the east end of this room, forty-nine feet four inches by sixteen feet eight inches, was the chair. . . . The floor of the room is cement, but a wooden flooring had been laid in the east end, and upon this the chair stood, screwed to the floor through rubber matting. The chair is the same that was used in Sing Sing. . . . The executioner's closet was in the southeast corner, and a gleaming row of lights about the metres and necessary switches on the outside suggested the death-dealing power. Lying across the arms of the chair was also a row of incandescent lamps on a board. . . . Warden Thayer left the room and in a moment returned followed by the doomed criminal walking between two guards. . . . Deputy McKenna took him by one arm and a hand and . . . urged him back in the death chair. . . . The straps were fastened and the electrodes applied to the head and either leg. When the mask was being put over his face, Wood muttered: "Don't hurry, boys." The feet were strapped, the arms were strapped, a band put about the waist and the mask was put over the face all in thirty seconds. As he seated himself, Wood exclaimed, in a clear voice: "God, remember me in heaven." . . . There was a movement of Dr. Ransom's arm that was hardly perceptible, and then Electrician Davis drew down the lever, sending 1,560 volts of electricity into the body. . . . The current was held on for twelve seconds and then the contact was broken, and the body lapsed into a limp condition. When eight seconds had passed the current was again put on and continued for ten seconds. There was the same spasmodic movement of the body; the hands, which had been clinched, turned palms and fingers opened. . . . The circuit was again turned off for twelve seconds and the body straightened up again. When the contact was made white vapor and smoke issued from where the electrode pressed against the right temple. It coursed upward, and the witnesses began to smell burning rubber. Six seconds elapsed, when the current was turned off. The smoke immediately ceased to rise, and in three seconds the current was put on again and the contact continued seven seconds. The man had been electrocuted.

Alvin "Sam" Pasco's grave is marked by a small, plain tombstone.
PHOTOGRAPH BY NIKI KOUROFSKY.

CHAPTER NINE

Manhunts

MAJOR JAMES CALL

"The killer of Patrolman Richard Pelkey has eluded all roadblocks and traps, apparently slipping through the dense, rugged woodlands like a phantom."

—*Niagara Falls Gazette,* September 25, 1954

When readers picked up their *Adirondack Daily Enterprise* on August 5, 1954, they got an eyeful of drama—three Lake Placid policemen had been gunned down just past midnight—and an urgent call for help. "Have you seen this man?" the front page blared. "The desperado sought in today's Lake Placid shooting is described as 5 feet, 8 inches tall, weighing 140 to 150 pounds, with black bushy hair and a thin moustache. He is about 35 years old. One report is that he walks with a slight limp."

The fugitive, dressed in a tan trench coat and jeans, was armed with a knife, a .22-caliber rifle, and a semi-automatic pistol. A thirteen-state police alarm was sounded, and roadblocks were thrown up on major highways and lonely roads. Locals were urged to call the police if they saw anything suspicious, but no one should try to be a hero. "There is no question that the man is desperate—and dangerous," the *Enterprise* warned.

The shootout capped off a month of frayed nerves in and around Lake Placid. Since early July there had been a series of break-ins at unoccupied vacation homes and even a botched armed robbery near serene Mirror Lake. Most of the burglar's grabs were of a practical nature—a portable radio, a change of clothes, a jar of peanut butter—although there was a report of a major jewel heist from the exclusive Lake Placid Club.

From the list of mostly household goods that were stolen, police figured the culprit was using the Adirondacks as a hideout, maybe from a major crime. The area offered a cover of thick forest, as well as plum pickings at swanky Lake Placid to carry a criminal through a sticky situation.

A break in the case came when a caretaker for Dr. Perkins, an Albany-area dentist, told police he thought someone had been squatting in his boss's cabin on West Valley Road from time to time. Investigators guessed that their man was living in the backcountry under blue skies, then using the vacation home as a shelter when it stormed. So they watched and waited.

Their hunch paid off in the drizzly early morning hours of August 5, when they realized the quarry was holed up in his rainy-day den. One of the officers radioed for Sergeant Dominic Valenze, who had a key to the cabin. When he arrived at the scene, Valenze and Patrolman Bernard Fell moved in, while patrolmen Richard Pelkey and John Fagan stood guard outside. After sweeping the first floor, Valenze and Fell proceeded down to the basement. That's where they found a man crouched in the shower. A desperate man with a pistol.

Valenze blasted the shower wall with five bullets; each missed its mark. But the fugitive had better luck. Fell was shot in the abdomen, and Valenze took shots to the arm and chest. Pelkey, who was coming down the stairs, was struck in the chest and leg. The gunman picked up Fell's .38 revolver and grabbed Valenze by the belt, using him as a human shield to flee the scene. Valenze and Fell took weeks to recover from their wounds; thirty-one-year-old Patrolman Pelkey died five days after the attack.

Cops quickly swarmed the scene, with Captain Harold Muller of State Police Troop B, out of Malone, spearheading the manhunt—an epic deployment that would include hundreds of police and volunteers, plus bloodhounds, a borrowed Piper Super Cub plane, and a National Guard helicopter brought in from Buffalo. The *Plattsburgh Press-Republican* reported that any locals wanting to pitch in were told to come on down to the stationhouse to sign up, provided they had a gun and some warm clothes.

Muller initially concentrated on a three-square-mile stretch of woods; by the end of the 104-day hunt, searchers had scoured millions of acres.

The posses ran drives like deer hunters, combing the backcountry in long rows. At the beginning, the epicenter of the search was bounded by State Route 86 and the Old Military Road, with armed men parked about every twenty feet along those arteries. But soon trackers were venturing deep into what's now classified as the High Peaks Wilderness, sweeping trails and lean-tos. Volunteer firemen from villages across the region were called in to help.

At the outset, their prey was only about three miles west of Lake Placid, in a lean-to cobbled together from a green poncho and some brown canvas. The camp was well hidden a mile or so behind the Saranac Lake Golf Club and well supplied with gear lifted from local camps. The *Adirondack Daily Enterprise* wrote that the spot was camouflaged behind "an almost uniform wall of pine." The fugitive spent the early days of the hunt hunkered down in the rain, listening to reports of the search on his radio. But after a few days he moved on.

Travel was slow in the backcountry, especially in the early 1950s, after a devastating windstorm downed acres of trees, leaving the snarled and forbidding Adirondack backcountry even more snarled and forbidding. The wanted man lived off berries and pilfered food, and he often went hungry. After his capture, he admitted that he ate garbage and drank vinegar at one camp.

Despite its size and scope, the hunt for the cop-killer never turned up much. Almost constant rain hampered efforts, stopping the bloodhounds' sniffers and obscuring the view from the sky. Searchers did find a frying pan and remnants of a fire near Heart Lake, in the eastern High Peaks. And the owner of a sled-dog kennel in the northern Adirondacks reported some missing meat. In Long Lake, a caretaker told authorities that there had been suspicious activity around a summer cottage, along with the theft of a bottle of milk and a pound of sausage. A canoe had been borrowed from another camp in the area, and a heavy coat and compass were lifted from a car. But a couple of the closest encounters came a bit farther north.

In September, the mystery man ventured out of the wilderness and into the village of Tupper Lake. He'd kept himself trimmed and shaved, and he was respectably dressed in stolen clothes. A well-groomed stranger walking the streets raised few eyebrows, though he did get some unwanted attention. He was questioned by a few officers around town, but chatted his way clear, and even managed to sweet talk sandwiches and cake from some kids in the park.

Then, on the evening of September 13, the highway superintendent for the town of Altamont, Raymond Brunette, stopped by to check on his camp near the Tupper Lake golf course. In the barn behind the cabin, Brunette found a sleeping bag and duffle. On the bag sat a German Luger (investigators would verify it was the weapon that killed Patrolman Pelkey). When Brunette started back to his car, he saw a shadow and raised his rifle to get a better look through the scope. But before the situation could blow up, a truck came along and the intruder scampered away. Brunette flagged down the vehicle and told the driver to get the police.

All at once, the attention of the massive search shifted to the area. Fresh roadblocks were placed between Tupper Lake and Long Lake. The *Tupper Lake Free Press* reported that bloodhounds tracked the killer to a nearby trailhead, but from there the perpetual rain washed away the scent. Searchers had been skunked again—except for commandeering the fugitive's supplies: the gun and bedding, plus clothes and boots, a hunting knife, a bit of food, and an Adirondack guidebook with maps.

Once hunting season began, the cops thought they could use the army of gun-toting woodsmen that would fan out across the region to their advantage. But even with all the extra eyes scouting millions of acres from Tupper Lake to Northville, there was still no sign of the quarry. The weather was turning cold, though searchers weren't confident that even the coming winter would flush the man out. "No telling how many cabins that guy could hole up in," admitted Captain Muller to reporters in early October. "He might be more comfortable than we are."

The search finally came to an end in November, thanks to William A. Gold, a reporter from Nevada who wired in a tip after a good-looking young man calling himself James Chandler Morgan was hauled in for a rash of burglaries around Reno. The suspect, known as the "Squeaky Shoes Burglar" for his less-than-quiet nocturnal visits, gave his address as Lakewood, Ohio. That bit of information caught the attention of investi-

Major James Arlan Call in happier days.
COURTESY ADIRONDACK DAILY ENTERPRISE.

gators, since it was only about ten minutes from the town where Marilyn Sheppard was brutally murdered that past July. But Gold's sleuthing soon turned their attention; the enterprising journalist spotted a newspaper clipping of the Pelkey shooting and subsequent manhunt among Morgan's possessions and notified Lake Placid authorities.

After fingerprints confirmed a match between the Reno robber and the Lake Placid cop-killer, Captain Muller flew in to take custody of Morgan, who was now known to be Major James Arlan Call, a twenty-nine-year-old combat veteran currently AWOL from a Louisiana Air Force Base. The captain told the *Adirondack Daily Enterprise* by telephone, "His fingerprints are the prints of the man we have been seeking. He looks like the man. He IS the man. We're got our killer. The manhunt is over."

At first, Call would admit nothing but the burglaries in Reno; he claimed he couldn't remember anything about his activities east of St. Louis. Muller reported that the suspect seemed "calm most of the time. . . . He's soft spoken, and thinks carefully before he says anything." But Call did agree to waive extradition and face the first-degree murder charges in New York.

Back in New York, in a downstate police barracks, Call finally broke, coming clean on months of burglaries and the Lake Placid shooting. Next he was taken to Ray Brook to be fingered by his surviving victims and then carted off to the Essex County jail. (He paid a return visit to Lake Placid on the journey there, enjoying a steak dinner at The Majestic, albeit handcuffed and under heavy guard.) Call got a breather from his cell to take state police on a nine-hour tour of the area, pointing out the various hideouts that played a role in his escape, as well as the spot in Tupper Lake where he'd thrown Patrolman Fell's revolver after the shootout. He had walked more than 300 miles in all, emerging from the woods in Northville, at the southern tip of Adirondack Park.

Though he was indicted for first-degree murder and a laundry list of lesser charges, Call pleaded guilty to second-degree murder alone and was sentenced to twenty years to life. On May 11, he was carted from Elizabethtown to the mental health hospital at Clinton Prison, in Dannemora. Ten months later he was transferred to Attica. He lived as a model prisoner, and after little more than thirteen years he was released. Call died in a 1974 car crash in Ohio.

But not everyone was convinced that the case was closed on Call's life of crime, including the man who led the search for Officer Pelkey's murderer. "I'll find out if it's the last thing I do," Captain Muller told the *Adirondack Daily Enterprise* after Call was captured. "It was something big he was hiding from."

That "something big" may have been the Ohio murder Reno authorities had initially questioned Call about. For years, audiences rooted for the wrongly accused Dr. Richard Kimble in *The Fugitive*, a television series and movie loosely based on the Marilyn Sheppard murder case. Could Kimble's elusive "one-armed man" really have been a serial burglar with a limp who tried to escape his horrific deed in the deepest corners of the North Woods? In *Tailspin: The Strange Case of Major Call*, former Federal Bureau of Investigation agent Bernard F. Conners connects some dots between that Ohio killing and the Adirondacks' longest manhunt. ➼

CHAPTER TEN

Murderers

HENRY DEBOSNYS

*"On [August 1], there was found in a lonely woods near
Essex, N.Y., and covered with leaves, the body of
a woman named Betsey Wells Debosnys."*

—The National Police Gazette: New York, September 2, 1882

No one can say for sure whether Betsey Wells, of Essex, was ever
a very merry widow. But she was definitely a good deal less jovial
after she married Henry Delectnack Debosnys in June of 1882.
Word was that the newlyweds fought regularly, and that the dustups
hinged on Betsey's refusal to hand over her sizable property.

Betsey wasn't exactly rich, but she did have a choice fifteen-acre
Champlain Valley spread. And the mother of four also had a bit of cash
put by from the settlement that followed her husband's untimely death.
He'd been killed in an accident at the Split Rock Ore Bed, a tragedy
that'd left Betsey a widow at thirty. Most folks figured it was the payout
from the mining company that had lured Debosnys to her side. Betsey
would meet her future murderer about a month before their wedding,
when her children brought him home to dinner.

The handsome stranger from Philadelphia—a painter by trade—could
whisper sweet nothings in six different languages and had a fascinating
life story. He regaled his new ladylove with thrilling tales from his time

in Europe and the Indian Territories; he even claimed to have survived a Confederate sabre at Gettysburg. Betsey was just about swept off her feet. But she maintained her footing enough to realize she should keep her settlement money safely secreted away. According to family lore, she stashed it in a tin-covered box hidden under a living room windowsill.

The widow Wells was right to be concerned. Her daughter Rebecca would later testify that her new stepfather demanded the deed to the family's homestead soon after the couple married. And Betsey confided to Rebecca that she was afraid of her husband—whose name was not really Debosnys—especially after learning that his first two wives had died suspiciously young.

The conman had had enough of wedded bliss within weeks. On the morning of July 31, 1882, he and Betsey climbed aboard their wagon, telling daughter Eliza that they were headed to Port Henry to pick up Debosnys's father, who was bringing fine furniture and horses. As they drove south on Lake Road, the pair was spotted by farmers Bill Blinn and Allen Talbot. Betsey nodded to Blinn in greeting, but the couple didn't stop for a neighborly chat. They hurried on to Port Henry, where they spent the night in Sprague's Hotel. The following day, after Debosnys's father failed to show, they headed for home.

Betsey never made it. Allen Talbot saw the couple drive by his Whallon's Bay property and, not long after, spotted Debosnys "skulking" about the forest with a white cloth in his hand. When Betsey's strange new husband left the scene—minus his wife—Talbot thought it all seemed pretty suspicious. So he partnered up with Bill Blinn to search the area. They followed spatters of blood into the woods, tracing a trail that looked like something heavy being dragged through the underbrush. At its end was Betsey's corpse, covered loosely in leaves. (Dr. Edward Atkins, who would examine the body, found two bullet holes in her head—which he ruled weren't fatal—and noted that her throat had been "cut windpipe to backbone.") Talbot and Blinn ran for the nearest telegraph, in Whallonsburg, to wire authorities.

The culprit was in less of a hurry. After he offed his wife, he took a leisurely tour of the area, pausing to tell anyone who would listen that he'd left his wife back in Port Henry to set up house for his father. His final stop was the post office, where he asked after his wife's mail. But word of his misdeed had already arrived, and he was restrained and arrested. A search of his person and wagon turned up Betsey's rings and pocket-book, as well as a bloody knife and two pistols, one with a couple of chambers discharged.

Debosnys was sent to the Essex County jail to await trial, which was set for the following March. He spent the long months drawing and writing prolifically—just not very well. The pages of ramblings that he left behind were bursting with bad poetry. In one elegy, "To My Poor Wife," he likened Betsey to a bug, and imagined her death a peaceful crossing: "She died like golden insect in the dew, Calm and pure."

He also amused himself by devising an intricate code, for which he offered no cypher, confident that the common rabble would find his puzzle irresistible. To further titillate the "ignorant peasant farmer[s] of Essex County," as he called them, he assured reporters that his secrets would be discovered after his death. (The code has never been broken. No great loss to humanity, I'm sure.) When the prisoner wasn't penning creepy verses or stringing together random symbols, he entertained visitors and staged fits, for which he was dosed with mercury.

One caller, a reporter for the *Troy Times*, made it his business to poke around for more corpses in the wife killer's cluttered closet. A promising lead was the young woman who was seen with Debosnys when he arrived in the area on his "yacht" (actually a ratty old boat with a rigged up sail.) She didn't stick around for long, and the scuttlebutt was that Debosnys had tossed her overboard as the couple crossed Lake Champlain. But that story wasn't going anywhere—the lady in question, a disenchanted house-keeper, had reappeared in Philadelphia by mid-August. Though he was absolved of the drowning, the newspapers down there had plenty to say about Debosnys. The *Philadelphia Times* called him "a lazy 'ne'er-do-weel' who loafed about the vicinity until forced by hunger to perform some manual labor."

The missing girlfriend scoop was a nonstarter, so the *Times* correspondent latched on to another sordid tale. The prisoner let him in on a little secret: his current sojourn in Essex wasn't his first. Debosnys explained that he'd worked in town as a painter about a decade earlier. At the time, he was staying in the same boardinghouse as Henry Lemaire, a French quarryman with no close friends or family. The lonely immigrant—who had accumulated a nice little nest egg—disappeared one day, leaving all of his belongings behind. Debosnys said that he was sure Lemaire had been murdered by the owner of the boardinghouse and speculated that the body could be found under that establishment. Authorities promised to investigate, though they doubted the "terrible charges made against a man who has heretofore borne a good reputation." They were right. The outraged proprietor produced correspondence from his former tenant, who was very much alive and living back in France.

Debosnys's trial opened on March 6, 1883, during a snowstorm that packed the town with about a foot of snow, though the wicked weather didn't keep the crowds away, especially not the local ladies. Unfortunately for his groupies, Debosnys wasn't much to look at when he stumbled into court. The *Essex County Republican* wrote that "a more repulsive being we have never seen arraigned. Small, weak, sickly, trembling, supported as he walked by the two officers, complexion sallow, countenance dejected, despondent, and whole demeanor cringing and cowardly." Whether these symptoms were the result of the mercury that had been administered to the prisoner or just a complete put-on, the reporter would "not presume to analyze."

Both the prosecution and the defense took Debosnys's right to a speedy trial seriously—the proceedings were over by the following day. There was perhaps more discussion of the defendant's wardrobe choices than was strictly necessary, and a digression about stepdaughter Eliza's sore finger on the morning of the murder, but, for the most part, the testimony was damning. Debosnys was seen leaving home with his wife and coming back alone. He was spotted creeping around the site where Betsey's bloodied body had been found. And a gory knife and discharged pistol had been found in his possession.

When Debosnys took the stand in his own defense, reporters had to struggle to hear his almost incoherent testimony. But they caught the gist of it: he swore he was innocent. Debosnys said he had spent the trip home from Port Henry drinking wine and whiskey—a lot of wine and whiskey—and he guzzled even more when the couple stopped for lunch that

While in jail awaiting trial, Henry Debosnys turned into a prolific if clumsy writer and sketch artist. His misplaced attention to detail (here in the ground cover and Elizabeth's clothing) paralleled Henry's uneven testimony in court.
COURTESY ADIRONDACK HISTORY CENTER MUSEUM.

fateful day. He finally passed out, and his wife was missing when he came to. (In an earlier statement to authorities, Debosnys mentioned that a Scottish drifter was on the road that day, and he had invited the scraggly gentleman to tip a glass of whiskey with him.)

The prosecution wasn't buying it. The district attorney brought witnesses that swore Debosnys didn't look like he'd just come off a bender, and he didn't smell of booze either. Even Debosnys's lawyer—a former district attorney appointed to the case—scoffed at the story. He took a different tack in his closing arguments, admitting his client's guilt, but suggesting that the murder happened in a fit of passion and was not premeditated.

It took the jury less than ten minutes to return a verdict of guilty of murder in the first degree; the sentence was death by hanging. The *Plattsburgh Sentinel* reported that, upon hearing his fate, Debosnys "wept bitterly."

The tears didn't last. After the trial, Debosnys made himself comfortable in what he called the "Jenkins Hotel"—in honor of his jailer, Sheriff

Rollin Jenkins—and whiled away his remaining days penning more prose and poetry. His themes swung wildly from serene meditations on death to bitter diatribes against his "oppressors." The rhetoric climaxed in grandiose threats: "When the sun is turned into darkness and the moon into blood . . . on that day, if it be in my power, I will send you the great fire of destruction . . . and many will die on that day of vengeance."

But it wasn't all lamenting and lashing out. Debosnys spent some long afternoons mimicking a menagerie of animals, and also worked up an autobiography that he handed over to reporters. The manuscript, which was written in the third person, described a dashing adventurer who volunteered for an impressive number of wars and joined more than one Arctic expedition. Debosnys said he'd been born on his uncle's plantation in Portugal in 1836, and he drew sketches of his ancestor's palatial homes, but he never did reveal his true name. He vowed that his "down fall will never reach a member of my family in this world!"

The gallows were thrown up in the jail yard on the eve of the execution. Debosnys held court with a crowd of reporters on his last night on earth, and guards said that the condemned man slept soundly. The morning of the hanging, April 27, 1883, he was allowed out of his cell to

Henry Debosnys drew this self portrait in his cell, three months before swinging from the gallows for the murder of his wife. COURTESY ADIRONDACK HISTORY CENTER MUSEUM.

examine his scaffold. The *Plattsburgh Sentinel* wrote that Debosnys "made his appearance in a very business-like way, ran hastily up the steps, and took in the situation at a glance. He tried the knot and requested that it be soaped more that it might slip more easily; he cautioned the Sheriff to have plenty of slack to the rope, and inspected carefully the trap on which he was to stand. In his conversation he laughed quite heartily, and in returning to the cell, bowed to the bystanders." The prisoner was decked out in new clothes, thanks to the $15 he received for selling his body—once he was done with it—to a Westport doctor.

The event itself was a semi-private affair, since audience members needed a pass from the sheriff's office to catch the show. But the group of seventy-five that scored front-row seats was dwarfed by the crowd that mobbed the common outside the jail, settling for a peek of the prisoner's head and shoulders before the trapdoor was triggered.

The *Sentinel* reported that a bit before noon Debosnys "ascended the scaffold with a firm step and independent air, taking his stand on the drop with precision." His voice was less firm—many spectators couldn't make out his final statement, though the papers pegged it as a protestation of innocence. The *Plattsburgh Sentinel* heard Debosnys argue that the blood found on his knife was not human at all; it was from a chipmunk he had recently killed. Then the hood was drawn over his head and, the *Elizabethtown Post & Gazette* wrote, "Sheriff Jenkins put his foot upon the spring and in an instant Henry Debosnys was hurled into eternity." (According to the doctor who paid for the privilege of dissecting the corpse, his death didn't come quite that quickly: the knot was placed too high on the neck and Debosnys died from strangulation, not from a broken neck.) When his body was taken down and inspected, the fine folks of Essex were shocked by the lewd tattoos that covered his limbs. The designs were, according to the *Gazette*, "revolting enough to make even the remembrance of one so vile disgusting to the minds of decent people."

Decent people can still be shocked by Debosnys, or at least by his skull, which is on display at the Adirondack History Center Museum, in Essex, along with the noose that hurled him into eternity. ⇥

Hangings in the Adirondacks

Since most county seats find a home outside the Blue Line, there were only four legal executions by hanging that occurred within the modern boundaries of the Adirondack Park.

Debosnys was the third—and last—man to be hanged in Essex County. The first was an unfortunate John Doe who got caught stealing while stationed at His Majesty's Fort of Crown Point in 1759. The second was James Bishop, another wife killer, who met his maker on March 17, 1843. The *Plattsburgh Sentinel* showed more sympathy for Bishop's actions than they did for Debosnys's "heartless and bloodthirsty" act, explaining that Bishop was "jealous of his wife, probably with just cause," and only killed her with a club in a fit of drunken rage. He then heaved her body over a cliff to make her death look like a tragic accident. That hanging also took place in the Essex County jail yard, but the viewing was a bit more difficult, with a fierce wind kicking up curtains of snow from a recent storm.

Edward Earl, yet another wife murderer, had the honor of being the only person ever hanged in Hamilton County. He was strung up on a borrowed scaffold on October 14, 1881. A thousand rubberneckers showed up at the Lake Pleasant courthouse that day, though only a handful were allowed near the action. Earl was cavalier about the proceedings. He's said to have written in a letter to a friend, "I have fifteen days and some hours to live yet. . . . and then there is to be some hanging done, i.e., a tightrope performance. . . . It is a new business to me. I have not the hang of it yet, and I have some misgivings about the results."

Lake George, in Warren County, almost had a hanging. In 1881—back when the village was known as Caldwell—George H. Willett, who ran a barber shop in Glens Falls, was convicted of killing his brother-in-law and sentenced to be hanged. (Willett, whose original name was Ouellet, may have been a victim of French-Canadian profiling.) He was lodged in Caldwell's Warren County jail and spent his final days building an intricate model of a church out of cigar boxes and other scraps. It was such a wonder that Willett was able to sell it for a tidy $425, enough to buy himself new legal representation and file for another trial. He was eventually acquitted, in 1883. His model, nicknamed "the church that cheated the hangman," was displayed at that year's Vermont State Fair.

CHAPTER ELEVEN

Murderers

ERNEST DUANE

*"The defendant committed a most atrocious crime. He
left an aged man miles out into the woods in November
weather, shot through the left hip, to die slowly by bleeding
and freezing, all for the small sum of $144."*

—Assistant District Attorney B. W. Kearney

The week before Thanksgiving 1928, Eula Davis trekked from his
remote cabin to the general store in the village of Speculator, about
five miles away. The sixty-year-old guide and caretaker was hearing
impaired, but that didn't stop him from catching up with his many friends.
He also replenished his supplies, paying for the load from a healthy roll
of bills. But flashing his cash that day turned out to be a big mistake for
Davis. It was the last time his neighbors saw him alive.

On Thanksgiving Day, another local guide and handyman, thirty-four-
year-old Ernest Duane, tracked down state troopers Lester Egelston and
Ralph Fitch to let them in on his terrible discovery: Eula Davis had been
shot dead at his Whitaker Lake cottage, where he worked as a caretaker
for the Brooks hunting camp. Duane said he'd hiked out that way to grab
a haunch of venison he'd strung in a tree and decided to visit his friend—
the man who had mentored him in his trade. He knocked and got no
answer, so he let himself in and found Davis dead on the floor.

When the troopers arrived at Whitaker Lake they were met by a ghastly sight. Davis had been shot through the hip, but he didn't die right off—and it was clear that his final hours hadn't been peaceful. The fatally wounded man had left a trail of gore as he crawled across the floor on that freezing day, toward the last traces of warmth from the dying woodstove. He'd tied a useless tourniquet of rags around his leg, below the damage, and draped the corner of a quilt across his body. He was able to pull a pillow under his head, but he didn't get around to writing his final goodbye, though police found a pencil near his hand.

Davis's body was carted back to town in a handsled, and Dr. Russell Warner, of Wells, had to wait until the corpse thawed to perform an autopsy. The cause of death was the gaping bullet hole in Davis's hip, a wound littered with fragments of the paper money that was now missing from his back pocket.

Townsfolk couldn't figure who would kill such a well-liked character, but the cops had a hunch. Something had seemed fishy about Ernest Duane's story from the first. Why would he have bothered to knock on Davis's door that morning, at the home of a good friend he knew to be deaf? Investigators put the word out to shopkeepers to report any marred bills that came into their tills. Before long they had what they needed: Duane had passed a stained ten-spot with two telltale holes in it at Robert Baker's Speculator store.

The police brought Duane in and, after seven hours of questioning, he finally offered a confession: On Sunday morning, November 25, he had walked out to Davis's camp. "On my way into Whitaker Lake," Duane recounted, "I figured that Davis had money, and as I got to thinking about it, I decided I would rob him of his money. When I opened the door in the front part of the cabin, Davis, who is deaf, stood with his back towards me. . . . I shot him in the left hip." Davis, Duane said, fell unconscious. So he searched his fallen friend, pulling a billfold stuffed with cash from a back pocket. Duane claimed that he threw the loot into the woods on the way back home, holding back only one ten dollar bill. Four days later he went back to the scene of the crime and found Duane lying dead.

"I then came into Speculator to get the troopers," he continued, "but they were out. . . . Then I went home and ate my dinner and came back to the troopers and told them. . . . I make this statement of my own free will because I want to get the murder off my mind. It has been worrying me."

Duane pointed police toward the spot in the wilderness where he claimed to have thrown the money. Though a battalion of cops searched the snow with rakes, they found nothing. And the next day, when a Gloversville photographer hiked out to capture Eula's now-notorious cabin, he found it had been completely destroyed in a fire. The *Gloversville Morning Herald* was quick to report that the structure was "believed to have been intentionally burned to wipe out evidence against the slayer," though the article did concede that the blaze could have been unintentionally caused by the policemen who used the cabin to cook their lunch during the previous day's search. But even with the crime scene annihilated, prosecutors still had plenty to work with, especially after a search of Duane's spread turned up the murder weapon and $134 dollars hidden in the rafters of his woodshed, each bill with two bullet-sized holes.

When Duane's trial started on April 30, 1929, the entire state was riveted by the drama playing out in Hamilton County's new backcountry courthouse, in the tiny town of Lake Pleasant. The *Gloversville Morning Herald* reported that during the trial "crowds lined every available inch of space and stood several deep in the entrance to the room. . . . One woman fainted away in the jam."

From the start, the outside press was dismissive of the residents of Hamilton, the least-populated county in the state by a wide margin. Much was made of the fact that the county judge and district attorney weren't actually lawyers—a New York Supreme Court justice and a neighboring county's legal team had to be shipped in to try the case. The *Syracuse Journal* called it a "borrowed court," and the *Albany Evening News* exclaimed over the "unfamiliarity of the inhabitants with things legal," describing the jury foreman as a "quaint, plain, rough woodsman." (The foreman, Harry Stone, would later write a scathing letter to the *Evening News* knocking the condescending coverage. Then, to prove his sophistication, he penned a thirty-one-stanza quatrain poem about the trial, with inspired rhymes like State/debate and Duane/insane.)

Assistant District Attorney Bernard Kearney, the lead prosecutor, had faith in the jury, especially since none of them seemed very much troubled by the idea of handing down a death sentence. The *Gloversville Morning*

Herald reported that, of the fifty-plus potential jurors questioned on the first day of selection, "only three or four had any conscientious objections to capital punishment." Besides, Kearney had an open-and-shut case.

The prosecution painted a picture of a calculating man who set out to kill Eula Davis for money, then schemed to cover his tracks. In his opening remarks, Kearney described the aftermath of the crime: Duane "went to a brook in back of his home where he washed the blood off the bills, returned, tied the bills up with a fish line and hid them behind a rafter in the wood-shed of his home." He introduced the defendant's damning confession, and troopers described their discovery of the stolen loot and the gun—a .30-30 caliber Savage rifle—that a firearms expert confirmed was the model that had killed Eula Davis. As a final nail in Duane's coffin, one officer testified that Duane had admitted "he was glad it was all over, that he hoped he would get the chair and that he was very sorry for his mother."

During the proceedings, the defendant listened impassively—the *Albany Evening News* called him the "calmest man in the courtroom." Duane was a short fellow and "rather heavy set for his height," according to the *Amsterdam Evening Recorder,* but "faultlessly dressed" in a black worsted suit and snappy blue tie, with his black hair neatly styled in a pompadour and his beard trimmed close. His wife, a teenaged bride of less than a year, did not appear at the trial. And Duane may not have been as calm as he looked. The *Evening Recorder* remarked that he obsessively twisted his fingers or twirled his ring. His forefingers and thumbs were "heavily stained with nicotine from incessant smoking."

Duane's state of mind wasn't just fodder for the newsmongers. The defense, led by Saratoga Springs lawyer Carl McMahon, hung its entire case on Duane's mental competency. McMahon said his team "concedes that Eula Davis was killed by a bullet fired from a .30-30 Savage rifle in the hands of Duane." But he vowed to prove that his client, who suffered from epilepsy and was "mentally abnormal," murdered Davis in a dream-like trance. To back that up, Duane's brother took the stand and outlined previous "spells." McMahon also submitted discharge papers from World War I that released his client due to epilepsy—"one of the worst diseases of the brain known to man." The condition was exacerbated, the defense argued, by "weeks of lonely tramping through the woods, during which sometimes Duane never saw another person."

McMahon alleged that troopers used coercion to drag a false confession out of Duane, and then he put his man on the stand to offer a new and improved version of events. Duane testified that he remembered nothing from the point when he stepped into the clearing around Davis's cabin on November 25 until he awoke that night from a nightmare in which he had murdered his old friend. It was only when he found Davis's money in his pocket that he knew it was true. "Duane didn't actually kill," McMahon assured the jury, "he only 'dreamed' the slaying." The press took it and ran, dubbing Duane the "Dream Murderer."

After the experts weighed in on Duane's state of mind—two backing up McMahon's argument and two debunking the sleepwalking defense—the case went to the jury. But within a few hours, the panelists filed back into the courtroom and informed the judge that they were at a standstill: nine favored convicting Duane of murder in the first degree, two were opting for a lesser degree, and one was bent on acquittal. New York State Supreme Court Justice Christopher Heffernan sent them back to work, pointing out the expense of the trial to taxpayers—the most costly Hamilton County had ever seen—and the relatively short time that the jurors had been considering the case. "Sometimes," he told them, "it is necessary to argue back and forth and fight it out among yourselves." It must not have been much of a scuffle; after a total of five hours the jury had agreed on a guilty verdict. Justice Heffernan cried as he handed down the sentence: "I have but one duty to perform. I have wished it would never come to me, but Mr. Duane you stand convicted of murder in the first degree, for which the punishment is death."

McMahon brought the case to the appeals court that fall, focusing on the early disagreements among the jury and the judge's instructions to the panelists. It didn't fly; Duane's sentence was upheld and his electrocution was set for the week of January 13, 1930, at Sing Sing. Then, the day before the execution, Governor Roosevelt commuted the sentence to life in prison, writing, "I cannot bring myself to believe that the state should visit the extreme penalty of death upon a man whom the government rejected from service because he was suffering from a mental disorder."

Duane soon discovered that he wasn't the only one granted clemency:

the chicken that was going to star in his final meal lived to cluck another day. The *Gloversville Morning Herald* reported that Duane was bitterly disappointed in the loss of his feast. Upon hearing word of his reprieve, he lamented, "I'll lose my chicken dinner, then." Duane died in prison some twenty years later. The ultimate fate of the pardoned poultry remains unknown. ➤

Boxing Days

In newspaper coverage of the Ernest Duane trial, both Duane and his victim were linked to heavyweight champion Gene Tunney. Some outlets pegged Duane as a one-time guide for Tunney; others said it was Davis who squired the boxing star around the wilderness. One writer remembered Davis hosting Tunney in his modest cabin, sharing food and woodsy wisdom with the champ.

Lots of townsfolk had a brush or two with Tunney's greatness when he spent summers training in Speculator between 1926 and 1928. The up-and-coming fighter had served in World War I with Bill Osborne, whose family owned the Osborne Inn. (Bill was William Osborne's son, see chapter 5.) Osborne assured his buddy that secluded Speculator would be the perfect place to train. So, when Tunney was facing his biggest challenge—a heavyweight championship matchup with Jack Dempsey in 1926—he took his friend's advice.

During Tunney's three summers at Speculator, the sleepy village was flooded with his well-heeled entourage, along with boxing fans and reporters (including a young correspondent by the name of Ed Sullivan). Tunney stayed in a cottage next to the three-story Osborne Inn and sparred in a training ring on the grounds, drawing thousands of spectators. He also ran the region's hilly roads and rowed on 1,500-acre Lake Pleasant to keep in top shape, telling one reporter that "all the natural advantages that contribute to build up one's body and mind are present."

After his first training season in Speculator, Tunney leveled Dempsey in ten rounds to become the new heavyweight champ. He successfully defended his title in 1927—a rematch with Dempsey—and again in 1928, against New Zealand strongman Tom Heeney, before retiring. Speculator hadn't seen the last of boxing greats, though—Max Schmeling and Max Baer would also take turns in its sparring ring

Ernest Duane's date with this electric chair at Sing Sing Prison was called off by Governor Roosevelt. PHOTOGRAPH BY T. FRED ROBBINS, COURTESY LIBRARY OF CONGRESS, LC-USZ62-35632.

Gene Tunney in 1934. PHOTOGRAPH BY CARL VAN VECHTEN, COURTESY LIBRARY OF CONGRESS, LC-USZ62-103685.

CHAPTER TWELVE

Murderers

CHARLES "MUSKRAT" ROBARE

*"With the passing of the Prohibition era, [Charles
"Muskrat"] Robare fell upon evil times. This means
of easy money taken from him, he turned to other
questionable occupations."*

—*Plattsburgh Daily Republican*, June 5, 1942

even hundred gallons, portioned out in five-gallon cans. That's how
much hooch the *Plattsburgh Daily Republican* reported was confis-
cated in a 1935 bust of Charles "Muskrat" Robare's mega-moonshine
operation, tucked away on a farm in the town of Chesterfield. According
to the *Ticonderoga Sentinel*, the haul was only thirty gallons of finished
product, plus mash, molasses and a giant vat of "first run" (the initial low-
grade output of a still). But the tally of wet goods was beside the point;
what really made the G-men smile was dismantling a 5,000-gallon still,
the workhorse that had allowed thirty-two-year-old Robare to corner the
region's illegal liquor market. (Although Prohibition was over, the demand for tax-free booze hadn't dried up.) State troopers called the still
the largest they'd ever found in northern New York; Alcohol Tax Unit
officers were credited with a seizure estimated at $15,000 to $20,000.

Robare and three other men who were hanging around the farm that day
were dragged into a federal courtroom, but only Muskrat came away with a

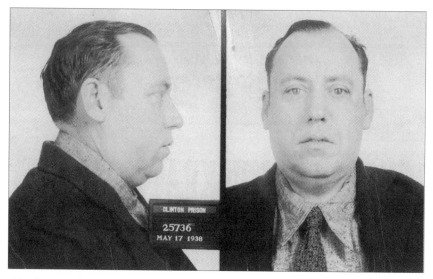

Charles "Muskrat" Robare, a heavy hitter on the North Country bootlegging scene, also spent time in Dannemora's Clinton Prison for cattle rustling. COURTESY OF THE PLATTSBURGH POLICE DEPARTMENT.

sentence—one year and nine months in a Pennsylvania pen and a $4,500 fine.

It wouldn't be the first time Robare had seen the inside of a jail cell. The Adirondacks, with its yawning wilderness only spitting distance from the Canadian border, was the perfect backdrop for bootleggers, and Muskrat Robare was one of their kings. Between 1927 and 1928, state troopers out of Malone nabbed Muskrat eight times for violations of Prohibition. (Word was that he earned the handle "Muskrat" after a heart-stopping aquatic escape from revenue men—but he was described as "squat" and "taciturn" in press reports, so the nickname might have had something to do with his looks and temperament.)

In 1931, Robare's need for a steady stream of new, fast cars brought him more unwanted attention from the law. That summer he was collared for passing a bogus $500 check to a car dealer in Au Sable Forks. Soon after, he was caught up in an investigation of a car-theft ring, nailed with a hot vehicle from New York City in his garage. He didn't spend much time in the slammer for either incident, but he did take a financial hit for the stolen ride, losing the $300 in cash and $600 in Canadian ale authorities claimed he had laid out.

Robare made the papers plenty—the *Ticonderoga Sentinel* called him "one of the most notorious rumrunners in the North Country"—but he stayed out of really hot water until the fall of 1931, when he pleaded guilty to conspiracy. Seems Robare and a gang of like-minded souls were slipping border patrol officers a good deal of money and beer to turn a blind eye to their antics. He netted a year and two months for the scandal, joining a couple of the disgraced officers in Atlanta's federal prison.

Muskrat was out on parole in less than a year, but not for long. In August of 1932 he was collared again, this time for smuggling some of his mountain dew into a little town near Montreal (in this porous border region, the illegal pipeline ran both ways). And his three-month sentence in a Canadian lockup was only the beginning of his troubles. After his time abroad, Robare was politely shuttled to the border at Rouses Point, where he was picked up by a deputy U.S. marshal and delivered to Leavenworth to finish up the sentence he thought he'd left behind in Atlanta.

His stints in jail didn't change Muskrat's wild ways, and even the end of Prohibition didn't slow him down. Wherever folks yearned to drink tax-free, Robare was there, ready to fill any outstretched glass. That is, until his super-still was shut down in 1935 and he was shipped back to prison. When that sentence was over, Robare finally had a change of heart. Or at least a change of plans: he settled down in Keeseville and decided to try his hand at cattle rustling. It didn't end well.

On a cold December night in 1937, Robare and two other reprobates borrowed a truck from a butcher in Plattsburgh and set out toward Lake Placid, with Robare following his friends in a car. At a farm in the town of North Elba, the bandits wrestled three cows into the back of the truck. But it was a long ride to the Clintonville woodlot where they planned to butcher the animals, and the vehicle wasn't quite up to the task. Robare had to leave the broken-down jalopy on the side of the road, with the three confused cows in the back, while he raced off to Keeseville to pick up another truck.

Soon the trio was reloading their ill-gotten cargo into a new set of borrowed wheels, securing the livestock with ropes. Except they weren't very secure. The second truck was smaller and, on the rough roads, one cow slipped out of the truck and got hung up on its rope. That's when the operation started to attract attention. Somewhere along the Wilmington Road, another driver noticed the animal's predicament and slowed down to help. The last thing Robare and his friends needed was a witness; they sped up, dragging the unfortunate cow along behind.

The *Ticonderoga Sentinel* called the resulting carnage—which they described in gruesome detail—"one of the most brutal acts of animal torture in the history of the North Country." Robare spent three years in Dannemora for his part in the affair, but he wasn't finished showing the North Country just how brutal he could be.

In the spring of 1942, while he was still on parole for the cattle-boosting disaster, Robare traveled to Plattsburgh to call on Yale Morris, a well-known meat dealer. The World War I veteran had built up his successful business after emigrating from Russia almost forty years earlier. He was a "man of regular habit," according to the *Plattsburgh Daily Press*, and most folks knew he carried a lot of cash with him on his trading trips.

Robare asked Morris—within earshot of the meat dealer's sister, Mattie—to come on out to the Peru farm he was sharecropping to check out a cow or two he had to sell. So the dealer stopped by the spread on the morning of June 1, and his host led him out to the grazing herd. Muskrat brought along an ax, a hammer, and some nails, supposedly to fix a fence in the back forty.

Robare would later admit, in a twenty-one-page statement, that he struck Morris with the flat side of his double-bladed ax that day, laying him out in the quiet field. ("The son of a bitch went down like a beef," he boasted to a state trooper.) Robare finished him off with a second blow. Then he riffled through his victim's pockets, taking a stack of bills from Morris's wallet, and hastily piled some leaves and pine needles over his dirty work. As he walked back to the farmhouse, he met up with his landlord, seventy-nine-year-old Michael Connell. "What did you do, kill the cattle buyer down there?" Connell joked.

Muskrat didn't stick around to explain. He handed his clothes over to his wife for cleaning and drove the meat dealer's vehicle back to Plattsburgh, where he abandoned the truck and hitched a ride back to the farm. Then he got busy re-stashing his victim in a more secure hiding place. He wrapped Morris up in canvas and used a rope to drag the corpse to a small hollow about seventy-five feet away, burying the remains under some brush and leaves. Then he hid Morris's gray cap beneath a stone along the path back home. Two days later, Robare was at W. W. Finney & Son trying to put a substantial down payment on a tractor he had been coveting. But the machine wasn't in working order, and Finney wasn't selling, even after his eager customer pulled out a roll of bills, saying, "I can pay you cash for the tractor today."

Morris was reported missing by his nephew on June 2, and his well-known Dodge pickup was soon recovered on Bridge Street—keys in the ignition, but no sign of its owner. Police suspected foul play from the first. Mattie knew her brother had set up an appointment with a seller, but she hadn't gotten the gentleman's name. She described him as "short and fat." So an officer visited another meat dealer, Harry Steinberg, who remembered that Robare had been making the rounds, looking to sell some cattle. A neighbor had seen Morris get into his cattle-hauling truck, a dark green half-ton with unpainted wooden sides, early that Monday morning, and another acquaintance had spotted him heading in the direction of Robare's spread.

When investigators questioned the career criminal, he played it cool at first, explaining that Morris had come and gone that morning, taking off to look at more head of cattle in Morrisonville. But after a dozen hours of interrogation, Plattsburgh Police Chief Clifford Fleming lulled him into a confession. "Everyone else had left the room," Fleming recounted in his deposition, "and Mr. Robare and I sat and smoked and talked about former days and times and people we knew back in prohibition days." Then the chief asked about Morris, and the suspect admitted he "hit him over the head with an axe." He showed no signs of emotion.

In the predawn hours of June 4, Robare led a parade of flashlight-wielding police, plus reporters, photographers, the coroner, and the district attorney, to the scene of the crime. He took his tour group to the bloody murder site, then gestured toward the camouflaged body. Officer Wilfred Trombley reported that Muskrat "laughed and joked" afterwards, seeming relieved to "get it off his chest." Cops would later uncover $370 in the horse barn, buried under chaff behind a grain box.

Robare claimed he and Morris squabbled over the cattle deal; he lost his temper and Morris lost his life. But the prosecution saw it differently and charged him with first-degree murder. District Attorney John Cummins insisted that the ex-con had lured Morris out to a lonely field under false pretenses—the cows on the Connell farm weren't even Robare's to sell—and crushed his skull for cash. With his lengthy confession, Cummins said, "Robare gave us a clear case of premeditated, cold-blooded murder," and the penalty should be death. Robare was lodged at the Clinton County jail to await his fate; Morris was lodged at the Beth Israel Cemetery.

The trial kicked off in early December. On the opening day of testimony, thirteen witnesses took the stand for the prosecution, including several who described that early morning fieldtrip when Robare pointed out Morris's concealed body. The coroner detailed how the victim's head had been "mashed in," and Chief Fleming recounted Robare's confession. A milk delivery boy was able to put Morris at the defendant's farm on the morning of June 1, remembering that the gentleman had wished him a "good morning." And the state trooper who rode with Robare to the scene of the crime after he'd confessed testified that he asked the suspect why

Grand Theft Auto

Because smugglers needed a constantly revolving inventory of fast wheels, bootlegging and car thievery went together like peas and carrots. Robare had been linked to a syndicate out of New York City, but there was also a prolific gang of automobile thieves right in his back-yard—what the Plattsburgh Sentinel called "the most active rum ring and car ring operating between Utica and this city."

In November of 1927, Sergeant Carroll, of Malone's formidable Troop B, got a tip that a bootlegging outfit was keeping a stash of hot rides in a Sciota garage, just ten miles from the Canadian border. Carroll raided the place and seized a couple of cars lifted from Utica, but his source assured him that the cache was just the beginning. His chatty friend—a rival rumrunner?—let him know that there were at least seven vehicles from Utica making daily hooch hauls from Sciota to Saranac Lake.

Within a few days, Carroll had snagged Lawrence Swinger racing through Plattsburgh in a stolen Hudson Brougham and Louis Grande he'd done it. Robare responded, "I expected the doublecross. . . . I've been double-crossed all my life, my relatives have doublecrossed me. There's one Jew son of a bitch who'll never doublecross anybody else."

The following day, Robare's hired hand took the stand, recalling that he'd been ordered off the farm that fateful morning, tasked with returning a corn planter to a neighbor. Then Michael Connell testified that his tenant had gone out to the fields with Morris and came back alone. Robare's wife, who some said wasn't feeling the Muskrat love anymore, backed up Connell's account—except her version of Connell's attempt at humor that morning swapped the word "Jew" for "cattle buyer." She recalled that she had washed her husband's clothes for him after he returned from the field. Later she noticed that both her husband and the meat dealer's truck were missing. The Rouses Point *North Countryman* reported that the defendant, who had seemed pretty calm and collected up to this point, looked uncomfortable during his wife's testimony, dropping his eyes and fiddling with a groove in the defense table.

At the end of the daylong parade of damning evidence—including the

cruising near West Chazy in a hot Chrysler. And those two were almost as accommodating as the original informant. Before long, Carroll and his men were surrounding the gang's headquarters, an unassuming chicken farm on Lake Flower Avenue in Saranac Lake.

Eugene De Crisci, Nicholas "Utica Nick" Nole, and his brother Michael were arrested in the roundup, which netted police three more stolen cars and a boatload of booze. But Nick Nole, who was on parole from Auburn Prison, wasn't interested in accompanying the cops to the station. He asked the officers if he could retrieve his coat, then took the opportunity to jump out of an upstairs window. The law didn't catch up with him again until August of the following year, when he surfaced at a Canadian hospital with a gunshot wound, courtesy of a lady friend.

De Crisci had his own reasons for not wanting to find himself in front of a judge (there were questions surrounding a stabbing incident in Utica that he was anxious to avoid). So he slipped out of his handcuffs and managed to stay lost for a spell—until police uncovered him in a Utica apartment and dragged him out, desperately clinging to the furniture, to face his fourth felony conviction.

defendant's signed confession, which was admitted into evidence over his attorney's objection that it was made under duress—Robare holed up in his cell. According to the *North Countryman*, he asked for a pack of smokes and ate a "hearty supper." In the morning he was scheduled to take the stand in his own defense.

As the guard made his regular rounds that night, Robare seemed to be sleeping the untroubled sleep of the innocent. The next morning he was up early, dressed and ready for breakfast by 5:45, presumably anticipating his big debut on the witness stand. But by his next circuit around the cells, at 6:05, the turnkey found the prisoner hanging from the iron grating above his cot. Seeing that his bill had come due, Muskrat had rigged a noose out of his belt and a towel to cheat the government one last time. ⇥

CHAPTER THIRTEEN

LAWLESS LADIES

"The publicity the defendant has attained in her exploits in this section, together with the novelty of a woman being on trial for burglary, supposed to be an exclusively masculine accomplishment, no doubt brought many spectators to the court house yesterday."

—*Plattsburgh Daily Press*, on the Florence Hilton affair, December 22, 1897

In the ranks of Adirondack scofflaws, Lucy "Mother" Johnson may be the most beloved. Early Adirondack travel booster W. H. H. Murray wrote that the hardy Raquette Falls hosteller nearly laid him low with the quality and quantity of her flapjacks. But whipping up criminally good pancakes isn't what brands her a rebel.

Photographer and guidebook author Seneca Ray Stoddard recorded Mother Johnson's naughtiness in his 1874 *The Adirondacks Illustrated:*

"What kind of fish is that, Mrs. Johnson?" I inquired.

"Well," said she, "they don't have no name after the 15th of September. They are a good deal like trout, but it's against the law to catch trout after the fifteenth, you know."

Not counting the woodswomen who filled their table with forbidden fish and game, there aren't many honest-to-goodness outlaws of the female persuasion strolling the pages of Adirondack history.

Maybe Adirondack womenfolk were too busy trying to survive to get very rowdy. Or maybe they were just better at not getting caught.

But Florence Hilton had plenty of time for shenanigans, and not enough sense to escape detection. The twenty-four-year-old got into mischief on October 30, 1897, when she broke into Coonley's general store in a hole-in-the-wall community aptly named Frontier, the last stop before the Canadian border in the town of Clinton. Once inside, she updated her wardrobe, grabbing about $100 in skirts and such, plus gloves, watches, and rings.

Unfortunately for the fashion-forward felon, witnesses spotted a woman leaving the area in some ill-gotten finery. Cops immediately suspected Hilton, who was "quite well known in police circles," according to the *Plattsburgh Sentinel*. (In June of that year she was sentenced to "thirty days reflection in the cooler" for what the *Plattsburgh Daily Press* delicately referred to as being "much in evidence about the garrison.")

Lawmen swung by the den the *Sentinel* called Hilton's "headquarters," a shack in the town of Dannemora, about thirty miles south of Frontier. But she wasn't home to receive callers; she was too busy getting arrested for "general carousing and cutting up" in Cadyville. Hilton was shipped off to Plattsburgh under the charge of vagrancy, but when the sheriff received the warrant for the Coonley's caper, the rap for licentious living was swapped out for burglary and larceny. Hilton didn't have much of a defense, since some of the pilfered frippery was found on her person.

She was given accommodations in the Clinton County jail until her late December trial, and likely her holiday season wasn't very jolly. At Hilton's court date in Churubusco, the *Plattsburgh Sentinel* wrote that she appeared frail as she gave her age, her unmarried status, and admitted to being "intemperate." She pled guilty to burglary in exchange for the prosecution dropping the larceny charge, then the judge made some small talk about the rarity of a female burglar before slapping her with a two-year, two-month sentence.

Hilton was delivered to the State Prison for Women at Auburn after ringing in the New Year back at the Clinton County slammer. The *Plattsburgh Sentinel* gave her a bit of advice as a parting gift, suggesting that she use her time away to learn the error of her ways and hoping that "she

Living in a rugged, remote landscape, many Adirondack women were crack shots, and not above bending the rules. COURTESY LIBRARY OF CONGRESS, LC-F8- 15707.

can be induced to refrain from going on the stage. A penitent burglar we can forgive, but a female burglar actress—never!"

Jessie Elliott, of Beaver River fame, was not eaten by her dogs. Honestly, that's not something I should have to clarify. But here we are. In his *A Short History of Beaver River,* Bill Donnelly writes, "Jess froze to death in her house and it is said that her three dogs, trapped inside with their mistress, fed on her corpse." And that's not even the worst piece of gossip about poor Jess Elliott. She was painted up as a whore in local histories, all on hearsay evidence filtered through the generations. Donnelly confides that Elliott was popular with the lumbermen come payday, adding, "On a busy evening the line might extend outside the house."

Well, now, really. Shacking up with three different men—two of whom she properly married—is a far cry from servicing every lumberjack within hollering distance. But before I get myself all wound up, maybe I should start at the beginning.

Jessie Elliott was born in 1885, daughter of Chester and Addie Elliott, who ran a popular boardinghouse in Beaver River. In the 1910 census, when she was just a quarter-century old, Jess was listed as divorced and unencumbered by offspring. That wasn't the only shocking snippet that marked her as a progressive woman. By all accounts, she dressed as a man, packed a pistol on her hip, and rode astride a black steed.

Before long, another fellow took a try at taming "Wild Jess Elliott." In 1913, she married Budd DeLong, a station agent and telegrapher for the New York Central Railroad. But by 1920 that marriage was also kaput, and Jessie was living with her (possibly common-law) husband Harry Smith. Jess and Harry were cooking up grub in a lumber camp down near Woods Lake and DeLong was living with his mother in Utica.

Jessie and her hubby were back in Beaver River in October 1923, when Harry made the newspapers for pouring whiskey in his café. A crack team of G-men had been called in to curb the wet and wild ways of the lumberjacks who were hunkered down in the area, and they had their eyes on ol' Harry Smith and hotelier Charles Ellerby as the source of all the spirits running through town. (The way the *Utica Observer Dispatch* described the settlement, the government shouldn't have begrudged the workers a drink or two: "With its rough, crude surroundings and several hundred French Canadian huskies living in tumble down shacks—or some of them with the bare ground for a bed and the sky for a roof, Beaver River didn't look like the 20th century and New York State.")

It didn't take any fancy detective work to close the case; officers posing as thirsty woodsmen just bellied up to the bars and their whistles were duly wetted. The businessmen were trotted off to court in Utica after Smith poured a snort of hooch for an undercover revenue man, and Ellerby topped him with two for a dollar. But headline-hustlers weren't interested in Harry and his troubles, not when there was a breeches-wearing, pistol-toting feral female by his side. The *Observer Dispatch* introduced Jess to their readers as a "Girl Rough Rider" who reigned as "queen of the camp" (although the "girl" was pushing forty).

This "daring cowgirl," the article explained, helped her husband supply the place with whiskey and was not the kind of character who cottoned to interference: "Mrs. Smith always has her pony near by and her six-shooter is fastened to her belt, where she can whip it out on a moment's notice. Needless to say the prohibition men let her alone."

Harry didn't learn his lesson after his first Volstead violation. In July of 1924, Smith's "lunch room" made the *Ogdensburg Republican-Journal* after a customer was nabbed sneaking out the backdoor with a couple quarts of booze hidden in a maple syrup can. (According to the *Adirondack Record*, syrup cans were becoming the container of choice for Beaver River bootleggers.)

But after that incident, the rascal Harry Smith faded from the news, and somehow he disappeared from Jessie's side as well. In 1928, at age forty-three, she died alone in Lewis County, possibly of a lung hemorrhage. Her body was found by friends about a week after she died. Contrary to the tall tales that circulated about her three dogs' banquet at her death bed, the *Watertown Daily Times* reported that the animals were almost starved by the time her death was discovered.

In 1924, a Miss Harriett Rega made a nice living in the fur market. Homesteading in a one-woman cabin in Old Forge, Rega set eighty traps in the Moose River and around Nicks Lake, reeling in raccoon, mink, and muskrat. The *St. Lawrence Weekly Democrat* and other outlets called her the only woman trapper in the Adirondacks. (The newspaper reports all but named her a freak show, exclaiming that she skinned the animals herself and did all the repairs on her cabin.)

Mildred Harris didn't want to work so hard for her fine furs. So, in October of 1938, she and a girlfriend wandered into Edelberg's Saranac Lake fur shop and posed as well-heeled visitors looking to add several choice items to their winter-weather wardrobe. They tried on a parade of merchandise, acting the part of indecisive customers while scoping the joint for the very best specimens.

A couple of days later, right before closing on a Saturday night, the women came back in and chatted up the clerk while their escorts loosened the lock on the door. Then, a bit before midnight, the gals breezed into the shop, leaving the gents to play chauffeur and lookout. In three or four trips, the cocksure culprits loaded piles of prime furs into their big green getaway car right in front of patrons filing out of the movie theater next door. At first, witnesses assumed Edelberg was making a late-night delivery. Then one nosy neighbor realized the car was all wrong and notified police. Once the authorities realized what was going on, they put up roadblocks on all the routes leaving the village, but the crooks had already slipped the noose.

The gang got away with $5,000 in coats and capes. At least initially. In less than a week, police had nabbed one suspect in Long Island, a gentleman the *Lake Placid News* described as a "sleek, swarthy man" who refused to flip on his fellows. The "emotionless and silent" Delio Bei was carted to Saranac Lake for identification by witnesses, then shipped off to the Franklin County jail in Malone to await trial.

In the spring of 1939, one of Bei's lady accomplices, Mildred Harris, alias Mildred Lewis, was unearthed in Illinois and brought back to the North Country to face first-degree grand larceny and third-degree burglary charges. But behind many a wayward woman stands a man ready to take the blame. In Mildred's case it was her bald and stocky husband, John Campbell, alias John Lewis, who pleaded guilty to everything in return for his stylish wife's release. He joined his friend Bei for ten to twenty years hard labor in Dannemora. The fourth fur filcher will forever remain a Jane Doe.

Running rum across the border during Prohibition was one of the more common bits of devilment women got up to in the North Country. Editors were especially interested if the bootlegging babes were pretty or famous—or both. In August of 1924, "bobbed-hair beauty" Anna Mayo, a vaudeville ingénue, was dubbed "Queen of the Bootleg Trail" by the *Lake Placid News* after her arrest in Lake George with twenty-three bags of Canadian ale. Though she blew a kiss at the U.S. Commissioner during her initial court appearance, she was eventually sentenced to thirty days in the Warren County jail for want of a $250 fine.

In 1925, Mrs. Clarence Parks was able to try some of that intoxicating excitement on for size without any of the repercussions. Mrs. Parks, who had helped her Prohibition-agent husband hunt down hooch manufacturers in the southern states, partnered with him again to run the North Country's rum trail in deep winter. They worked undercover as a boozy Bonnie and Clyde to sniff out bases of illicit operation along the way. She confided that her "first thrill came in Plattsburgh, when we dined in a hotel with one of the most prominent bootlegs in the north and his wife."

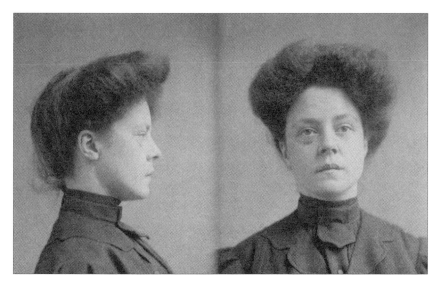

A mug shot is almost never flattering. Even with the latest hairdo, the portrait's sure to be spoiled by the black eye. COURTESY LIBRARY OF CONGRESS, LC-DIG-PPMSCA-10790.

On their smuggling outings, the couple was stopped here and there by curious officers, including a pair on horseback in Elizabethtown, but managed to talk themselves clear. Mrs. Parks said her biggest fright didn't come from carrying loads of illegal liquor past state troopers or mixing with mobsters; the real test was trying to crest gnarly Adirondack hills in the middle of a howling blizzard. "We skidded into ditches several times and were saved from injury by railing, or stopped just in time to avoid going over embankments."

"Trapping moonshiners in the hills of Georgia is nothing compared with running rum over the bootleg trail between the Canadian border and Albany," Mrs. Parks said. It may have been rough going, but it was productive. The couple's sleuthing netted fifty-five perps from thirty hotspots between Plattsburgh and the Capital District. In Plattsburgh alone, eleven men were collared and $50,000 in liquor was seized. Matthews' Garage in Chestertown was another big loser; Matthews and three of his employees were busted with a couple dozen five-gallon cans of alcohol and 232 bottles of Canadian ale. ⌖

CHAPTER FOURTEEN

Unsolved Mysteries

NORTH RIVER STAGE ROBBERY

*"The route of the coach from North Creek Station is
through an ideal stretch of country for a hold-up. Few
people make their homes there, and the whole face of
the land is of the wildest description."*

—*New York Times*, August 15, 1901

I magine a stagecoach robbery: a brown, dusty trail under the hot
Western sun, tumbleweeds bouncing through a forgotten town. Now
change out the backdrop for an Adirondack landscape, sparkling blue
lakes framed by cool, green forest. It seems incongruous, but the North
Country did echo with the call to "stand and deliver"—at least a few
times, anyway.

At the very start of the 1900s, a masked bandit waylaid the Agnew
stage as it rumbled between the resort towns of Lake Placid and
Elizabethtown. The coach had just made its usual pit stop in Keene,
a handy spot to get some grub and change the horses, and was starting
up the formidable Spruce Hill—at two punishing miles, really more of
a mountain than a hill. Since the best place to hold up a team of horses
was on a steep hill, where the beasts were slowed by their burden,
the conveyance had just entered into prime outlaw real estate.

The North River Hotel, where the targeted coach stopped just before its run-in with the mysterious masked man, was the go-to lunch stop for North Creek to Blue Mountain Lake Stage riders. PHOTOGRAPH BY SENECA RAY STODDARD, COURTESY OF THE ADIRONDACK MUSEUM, BLUE MOUNTAIN LAKE.

About a mile up the slog, the gunman stepped out of the brush and called for the driver to stop. He quickly relieved the unarmed occupants of their valuables and grabbed the mailbag before melting back into the woods. Between the driver and the deep-pocketed passengers, the culprit made away with several hundred dollars, not counting the watches and jewelry. He was never collared. The *New York Herald* called it "the richest haul ever made by a stage robber in the North Woods."

About a decade later, a Concord coach led by four lily-white horses was hauling twenty-five guests from the Paul Smith's depot to White Pine Camp, the Osgood Lake vacation home of filthy rich businessman Archibald White. The Fourth of July bash they were headed to was set to be the social event of the season, but the crew didn't make it to their posh party without incident. It was slow going on the sandy track, and the would-be revelers were easy pickings for a highwayman. But it wasn't just one gun-toting rascal that waylaid them about three miles down the trail—it was a wild pack of fifteen masked men and painted-up "Indians" that swooped toward the startled guests, whooping and firing off rounds (the *New York Times* would report that the gang was "scandalously wasteful of their powder"). The driver was tied up, as were the male passengers, and the bandits set about emptying pockets. In the middle of the fray, a sharp-eyed young woman noticed the gray-whiskered ruffian who was rifling through her purse was actually her host in a false beard.

White came clean to his guests—and, later, to a reporter from the *New York Times*. He said he planned the gag "as a novelty for my house party." And he couldn't resist parading out the old joke about hotelier Paul Smith's effect on vacationers' finances: "I did not make the same mistake that some real bandits made some years ago. They held up a coach load on their way home from a Summer spent at Paul Smiths. Of course the bandits found nothing. I planned my holdup better. I stuck up the coach load on their way in, when their pocketbooks would be well filled."

White's prank may have made the *Times*, but the most famous Adirondack stickup happened on August 14, 1901, in teensy North River, about five miles from the North Creek train station.

Around the turn of the twentieth century, North Creek was a bustling hub—at least by Adirondack standards. Packs of tourists, who were still eager for a taste of what outdoorsman William H. H. Murray had named a "Sportsman's Paradise" decades earlier, chugged up from Saratoga Springs on the Adirondack Railway. They disembarked at North Creek, and from there boarded the North Creek to Blue Mountain Lake Stage, aka the Red Ball line, which brought travelers to the very heart of the park via the artery that is now State Route 28.

On that August day, seven travelers—four men and three women—did just that, arriving in North Creek on the 10:30 train and boarding a Concord stage from Waddell's livery, with veteran driver William Eldridge at the reins. The party took a break from their eight-hour trek about five miles in, stopping at the North River Hotel for a bite to eat. Although some newspapers gave Dunlap's hostelry as the luncheon site, Will Eldridge's niece maintains that that was unlikely, as Dunlap's was a more rough-and-tumble establishment.

Back on the road, as the four horses hauled the rig up thickly wooded Coon Hill, about a mile outside of North River, a masked man in a slouch hat stepped out of the forest and leveled a Winchester rifle at Eldridge. The *Syracuse Evening Telegram* wrote that what happened next added even more of a "spice of adventure" to the Adirondack vacation scene. But the real adventure is teasing fact from fiction in the flood of newspaper write-ups that followed.

The barebones tale is that the desperado—a short, thick-set man, according to the *New York Herald*—yelled for the stage to stop. When Eldridge didn't pull up quickly enough, the highwayman fired at the horses, killing one of the leads. The shots spurred the driver and passengers into action: they got busy protecting their assets. Eldridge, depending on whom you believe, either tossed his employer's cash into the underbrush, or took to the woods himself, in order to hide the hefty bundle more effectively. Three of the four gentlemen passengers also hightailed it for the bushes. The fourth, a Mr. Marquette, stuffed hundreds of dollars down his pants, leaving only chump change behind for the robber to find. The women were overlooked in favor of the bulging mailbags (which yielded nothing of value), but some accounts include a feisty gal from Indian Lake who refused to be ignored—she supposedly gave the highwayman a good dressing down for killing the horse. A wagon coming up the road scared him off before he could make a more thorough search; his derring-do netted him about $20.

Once word of the holdup hit the wires, detectives rushed to the scene and a posse was rounded up to scour the region. But the culprit made a clean getaway, leaving behind only his hat as souvenir.

Not everybody was convinced that the crook was gone for good. In late August, the *Warrensburgh News* suspected that he was still hiding "near the scene of his daring exploit." They pointed toward the testimony of a youngster who swore he saw the man about a quarter of a mile from Dunlap's. The boy had been riding his bike toward North Creek when a stranger leaped from the trees and pointed his gun at him. The lad fell from his bike in surprise, busting a wheel in the tumble. By the time he had picked himself up and collected his wrecked ride, the gunman was gone. The *News* insisted his story carried weight, "as he is a truth telling boy."

Only days after the initial holdup, the *Hamilton County Record* broke the news that a trio of berry pickers stumbled upon a snoozing suspect as they were filling their buckets above North Creek. The stranger jumped up and covered them with his gun as he backed slowly into the wilderness.

But the *New York Times* sniffed, "No importance is attached to their story." The *Times* wasn't in any position to criticize. Their initial coverage put two highwaymen, not one, on that lonely Adirondack highway. And their reporting favored poking fun at the male passengers over uncovering the facts. As soon as the coach stopped, according to the *Times*, three of the men took "French leave from the stage." A fourth fellow was stopped from fleeing the scene only when "his wife grabbed his coat tails and delayed his progress." After emptying out purses and pockets, and tearing through the mail pouches, the *Times* initially totaled the take at more than $1,000.

The *Syracuse Evening Telegram* also got a little carried away with the tale, announcing on the front page that "there may be a lynching near Blue Mountain soon." The *Telegram* put a baby on board, a "black eyed little one" cuddled in her mama's arms. Their version is by far the most thrilling telling, complete with action and dialog worthy of the silver screen. The coach groaned as it rolled up Coon Hill; the baby's mother shrieked as she realized their peril; the horses "kicked and plunged." The male passengers, the *Telegram* reported, were ordered, "Come down from there one at a time and fork over." But the masked man was solicitous of the ladies, telling the mother, "Don't trouble yourself, Madam. I don't want your money." He touched his hat to her when his dirty work was done and sauntered off into the woods.

Not satisfied with just painting a romantic scene, the *Telegram* also offered a few suspects for their readers' consideration. One scenario—often repeated in other publications—blamed the caper on a stranger who had spent the night at Dunlap's and had taken off that morning armed with a rifle and a fishing rod. Another possibility was a man who had been staying in North Creek for a month or more and was fond of wearing a wide-brimmed hat very much like the one found at the scene of the crime. He had since disappeared and there was a rumor that a fellow matching that description was spotted heading south on the Adirondack Railway. Then there were the mysterious youths who had been lingering around Coon Hill for well on a week. The group was thought to be camping, but, the *Telegram* pointed out, "no one appears able to locate their camping rendezvous."

The wordsmiths at the *Hamilton County Record* threw in their two cents, labeling the culprit a "maniac." They noted that a "mentally unbalanced" character had been loitering about the area in recent weeks, staying in a few different area boarding houses, including Dunlap's. And the *New York Herald* speculated that he may have been a serial stickup man. About a week before, according to the *Herald*, a wealthy tourist was accosted in the same area and relieved of $400. News of this earlier robbery, the article explained, had been "suppressed by landowners of the vicinity."

Months after the incident, with the outlaw long gone and leads drying up, local dailies reported that the owner of the North Creek to Blue Mountain Stage, W. R. Waddell, had his own theory about the holdup. He suspected that the robber had planned to shake down William Moore, manager of the Barton Garnet Mines, on one of his trips to the worksite, but changed course when he realized Moore carried little cash. The stage carrying the payroll for workers on the Indian Lake Dam made a better target. But the criminal mastermind got his dates wrong—although local lore is split on whether the payroll was delivered the day before or after. Still, Mr. Waddell claimed that the passengers on his stage that day were carrying about $3,000, all told. It was their quick thinking (or speedy getaways) that kept the robber's take so low.

A descendant of William Waddell—another William Waddell—did his best to solve the mystery decades later. In a 1972 article for the *North Creek News Enterprise*, William Waddell the younger wrote that he had "spent much time . . . getting the facts together," and concluded that the culprit was indeed the stranger who had left Dunlap's earlier that day. The man had been a frequent guest at both Dunlap's and the Casey House down the road, using different names at each. Proprietor Jim Casey even played dominoes with the "nice fellow," who, he later noted, had some peculiar interests. Casey said his guest often rode the stage back and forth to Blue Mountain and Indian Lakes, keeping close track of the schedules— and especially noting payroll deliveries.

Did this harrowing holdup put a dent in the Adirondacks' robust tourist trade? Not according to the *Gloversville Daily Leader*, which reported that the notorious robbery was a boon for area businesses, bringing scores of gawkers to the scene of the crime.

The new Raquette Lake line travelled about eighteen miles, from the New York Central Railroad's Clearwater Station to the shores of Raquette

A passenger-laden steamer plies the waters of Blue Mountain Lake, circa 1911.
COURTESY LIBRARY OF CONGRESS, LC-USZ62-70981.

Lake, where vacationers could board a steamboat and cross to the Marion River Carry Railroad. "Railroad" is a generous term for the Marion River Carry setup, which may have been the smallest standard gauge railroad in the United States. Its tiny locomotive and three open trolley cars carted passengers less than a mile to Utowana Lake, where they could sail to Eagle Lake and, finally, enter Blue Mountain Lake. Fred Hodges, author Maitland DeSormo's father-in-law, called the scenic steam across Blue an "unforgettable and all-too-short trip." ⇥

Steamboats, Trains, and Stagecoaches

Seven passengers on the North Creek to Blue Mountain Stage was a light load for high summer—Mr. Waddell's chariots could carry up to fifteen. But Waddell had some serious competition once the Raquette Lake Railroad opened on July 1, 1900. Its raison d'être was shuttling fat-cats like Collis P. Huntington and William West Durant to their sprawling Adirondack camps in comfort. But the new tracks also gave less spectacularly wealthy vacationers another way to access the central Adirondacks, a preferable option to the interminable steamboat and buckboard tag-team tour up the Fulton Chain of Lakes or the jouncing stage ride from North Creek.

CHAPTER FIFTEEN

Unsolved Mysteries

LAKE GEORGE TROLLEY CAPER

"Dazzled by charms of an attractive and vivacious woman detective, who shrewdly planned his undoing, young Hawley became entangled in a web of suspicion which resulted in his arrest."

—*Warrensburgh News*, October 19, 1916

I n the early fall of 1916, as war raged in Europe, twenty-six-year-old H. Bernard Hawley was having a high time in the hopping tourist hub of Lake George. Hawley was not a romantic figure, simply a laid-off clerk for the Lake George post office, son of former postmaster Fred Hawley (father Fred would later become the mayor of Lake George). But he had still managed to snare the attentions of a free-wheeling young lady—an attractive stranger in town who was partial to wine and whoopee —and Hawley was making the most of this fortunate turn of events.

He had met Miss Agnes Elliott at one of his usual haunts, the Fort William Henry Hotel pergola, when she approached some of his friends and indicated she was a little bored with the scene, and that she would love to find a fine-looking gent with a car who knew how to show a gal a good time. Hawley heard the news and came running. Soon the two were inseparable, with Hawley squiring Elliott around town in his automobile, taking her to the richest resorts and sparing no expense. (Hawley's steady

Guests relax on the veranda of the Fort William Henry Hotel at Lake George.
COURTESY LIBRARY OF CONGRESS, LC-DIG-DET-4A25301

girl, Bertha Bentley, wasn't around to object—she was still recovering from injuries sustained from a fiery car crash. Hawley was at the wheel, but came out of the ordeal healthy enough for some high-stepping with Agnes Elliott. The long-suffering Miss Bentley would marry Hawley six years later.)

When it was time for Elliott to head home at the end of the season, Hawley offered a ride south with a bonus: a side trip to New York City for more shenanigans. The couple motored to Nyack, about thirty miles north of the metropolis, and proceeded to paint that town red. The *Warrensburgh News* tittered, "They registered separately but occupied adjoining rooms."

Hawley and his girl soon skipped over to New York City for another night to remember. But once they were resettled at the St. George Hotel in Nyack, recovering from the effects of their latest jag, Hawley was rousted out of bed by some rather insistent detectives. The dicks hauled him out of his love nest and into jail, charging him with a $30,000 heist back in Lake George. (But, the *Warrensburgh News* noted, not before Hawley paid the tab for both rooms, "while an inspector stood on either side.") Hawley's lady friend wasn't just another pretty party girl, she was a post office inspector who had been angling for a whispered confession among his sweet nothings.

The newspapers went wild, with headlines like "Postal Clerk Is Duped by Woman Sleuth" and "Delilah Traps Robbery Suspect." And the text was just as titillating as the headlines. With a wink and a nudge, the *Warrensburgh News* informed readers that the friendship between Hawley and Elliott "developed rapidly," and the *Syracuse Herald* added that, in the line of duty, Elliott "permitted him to make ardent love to her." (Get your mind out of the gutter. It didn't mean that back then.) The pair even registered as man and wife at one hotel, according to a scandalized *Poughkeepsie Evening News.*

The case that had Miss Elliott going above and beyond the call of duty involved the disappearance of a money-packed mailbag from a Lake George trolley en route to Glens Falls. The pouch, loaded with about $22,000 in cash and $8,000 in securities, had been stashed in the rear

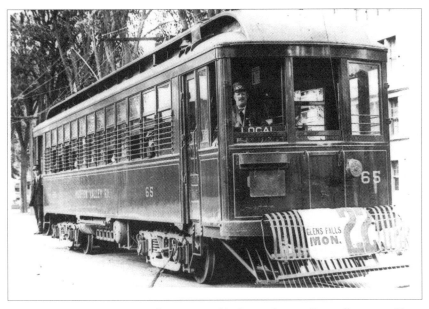

On the evening of August 22nd, someone robbed a Hudson Valley trolley not unlike this one en route to Glens Falls. COURTESY JOSEPH A. SMITH COLLECTION.

vestibule of a Hudson Valley railcar around 7:30 on the evening of August 22, an operation overseen by the postmaster and officers of the First National Bank of Lake George. The loot was on its way to an exchange bank in New York City, but it didn't get very far—the crew noticed the bag was missing by the time the train reached French Mountain, a scenic peak just south of the village. All that was found was the empty sack, abandoned along the railroad tracks.

The authorities' attention quickly turned to Hawley, who seemed to be living a bit beyond the means of an out-of-work postal clerk. The *Ticonderoga Sentinel* reported that Hawley partied it up at local hotels the day after the delivery was snatched, "his money flowing as freely as the champagne purchased." But, appearances aside, investigators had no real proof of Hawley's involvement. So they trucked in their bait, a "lady detective" who worked post office cases.

Elliott kept a careful log of Hawley's expenditures—down to the price of a pair of shoes—but she never did get that confession (though that didn't stop the *Sentinel* from publishing a rumor that Hawley had spilled the beans to his lady love in a drunken stupor). And the investigators who grilled Hawley in the hours following his arrest also struck out, even after telling the suspect that three others had already confessed and implicated him in the crime. (They hadn't.) The *Warrensburgh News* assured readers that the suspect had withstood all of the "brutal methods employed to wring a confession." Still, Hawley was arraigned in federal court in New York City and spent the weekend in the Tombs.

Investigators believed that Hawley had been tipped off about the major dough delivery by bank workers in the know. And in a public statement they theorized that the theft happened when the conductor stopped at a power station on the south side of the village (a spot some outlets reported was suspiciously close to the Hawley homestead). Another possibility investigators were trying on for size was a scenario where Hawley boarded the railcar that evening and kicked the moneybag off the train, allowing an accomplice to scoop up the loot from the side of the tracks. But all the fed's men couldn't find Hawley's supposed stash of cash—not in a bank account, and not squirreled away in any of the places he frequented.

Locals weren't surprised the authorities didn't get any goods on Hawley. He was a hometown boy from a good family, and there weren't many that were buying into the idea that he'd hijacked the mail pouch. (Miss Elliott came off less favorably around the neighborhood, painted up in news reports as a conniving viper.) After his arrest, the *Warrensburgh News* insisted that "Hawley is innocent," noting that the native son had never "laid himself open to a suspicion of dishonesty." The whole situation, the article explained, was a politically motivated frame-up. Young Hawley had just begun to dabble in politics, becoming a protégé of assemblyman Harry Brereton, a Republican powerbroker who just happened to be gearing up for an election. Hawley himself had recently won a spot on the Warren County Republican Committee after what the *Warrensburgh News* labeled a "bitter fight." A newspaper in Philadelphia picked up the story, pointing to the case as a "scandalous example" of the abuse of power by police.

Conspiracy or no, authorities stuck by their collar. Hawley was released on $5,000 bail while the U.S. attorney worked to scrape together some credible evidence against him. The government's case was brought before a federal grand jury in December and Hawley was indicted for theft, even though the prosecution had to resort to putting a downstate bellboy on the stand. That star witness testified that Hawley ordered a boatload of champagne and tipped generously when the now-notorious couple stayed at his hotel. Hawley spent Christmas Day in jail before being released on $25,000 bail, a tidy sum fundraised from some of the cream of Lake George and Glens Falls society. The judge defended his decision to increase bail from the previous $5,000, explaining, "If a man can steal the sum mentioned in the indictment and get away by forfeiting bail, it would be a profitable transaction."

From there the case sputtered and stalled. Investigators, for all their trouble and expense, failed to uncover enough evidence to bring Hawley to trial. And the suspect didn't help their efforts at all, keeping his nose clean and cooperating fully with the investigation. He made himself available for cross-examination and offered witnesses that swore he was at the Fort William Henry Hotel on the night of the robbery. According to the *Warrensburgh News*, Hawley was adamant that he could "account for every dollar of the money he spent on his excursions with the dashing detective."

When Hawley was drafted into the Army, in 1917, friends and neighbors figured he could finally put the ugliness behind him. He served in Europe and was honorably discharged at the close of hostilities.

But hostilities were still alive and well back home. In June of 1919, the feds dragged Hawley back into court—and this time they added his brother Harold and friend Burton McCormick to their guest list. After about forty witnesses from the Lake George area testified before the grand jury, the three were indicted for the moneybag theft, and McCormick was also nailed for perjury for a little white lie he let slip during the initial investigation in 1916. They all pleaded not guilty and were released on bail.

The *Gloversville Morning Herald*, for one, was indignant at the revival of the charges. "People who know the young man have always felt confident that he was not implicated," they wrote, pointing out that "the government has never pressed the case against him for trial, although at several times his counsel has demanded that he be tried or discharged."

And the government never did get the case to trial. In June of 1922, after a new U.S. attorney took over and looked into the affair, the charges against the brothers Hawley and Burton McCormick were dropped. Bernard Hawley's prospects hadn't suffered from the scandal; that fall he was appointed clerk for the Warren County juvenile court. He went on to become a leading citizen of Lake George, the owner of the popular Delevan Hotel and an executive of the Lake George Ice Company. He also served as a village trustee and spent his free time promoting winter harness racing on the lake. The *Ticonderoga Sentinel* called him "one of Warren County's best known businessmen."

But along with all his successes, Hawley really did have some crummy luck. Back in 1913, before his fifteen minutes in the spotlight with his dashing lady detective, his wrist and forearm were badly fractured in a freak car-cranking incident. That same year, he made the papers when a worker at a local garage took his Overland for an extended joyride. In 1915, he missed a turn and smashed his Peerless Motor Car into a telegraph pole, and the following year his future wife had to leap from his burning automobile. Hawley's Lake George restaurant was leveled in a fire in 1930; four years later, his Delevan Hotel was slightly singed, and then a nightclub on Beach Road that he held a stake in burned. He witnessed a

The pergola at the Fort William Henry Hotel, where H. Bernard Hawley first met Agnes Elliott. COURTESY LIBRARY OF CONGRESS, LC-D4-72671.

horrible motorcycle accident that killed a policeman in 1935. And finally, in 1937, the forty-eight-year-old's life was cut short when an Adirondack Transit Lines bus shuttling tourists from New York City to Saranac Lake skidded on a wet roadway and hit his car head-on.

The case of the Lake George trolley heist remains unsolved. After Hawley and company were exonerated, the *Glens Falls Post Star* wrote that "post office inspectors . . . have never succeeded in clearing up the mystery of when or how the mail pouch was stolen, or who were the guilty parties." Bernard Hawley may not have lifted that sack of cash off the trolley, but that doesn't mean he didn't have the last laugh on the government. After all, he was treated to a fabulous romp in the fall of 1916, courtesy of the United States Post Office and their kind loan of a good-time companion.

In *The Great and the Gracious on Millionaire's Row,* Kathryn O'Brien sets the scene on the pergola, where the charming postal detective first snared Hawley's attention: "Here, framed in colonnades and arches, [a visitor] could catch vistas of the lake, order refreshments from a hovering waiter, or, finding a partner, dance to the strains of the resident orchestra. He, or probably, she could stroll through a block of exotic shops that edged the lake and were accessible from the pergola, finding rare and expensive articles for sale." ⇥

Lakeside Living

When Thomas Jefferson clapped eyes on Lake George, it was love at first sight. In 1791, he wrote, "Lake George is without comparison, the most beautiful water I ever saw." And he didn't get much argument.

When Bernard Hawley was young and frisky, the southern Adirondack waterway was already known as the "Queen of American Lakes," and it was swarmed every summer by thousands of tourists—many with a good chunk of change in their pockets. There was plenty to keep them occupied: swimming, golfing, dancing, steamboat rides, or strolls out to Fort William Henry Hotel's fashionable pergola, which stretched out over the lake. The hotel, named for the nearby French and Indian War flashpoint made famous in *The Last of the Mohicans*, occupied a piece of the ten-mile stretch of lakeside real estate known as Millionaire's Row.

CHAPTER SIXTEEN

Unsolved Mysteries

THE ORRANDO DEXTER MURDER

"The motive for the crime was revenge for some real or fancied wrongs suffered by somebody who may have believed he was doing a righteous thing, for the benefit of the community at large."

—J. P. Badger, Esquire, from the *St. Lawrence Republican*, September 23, 1903

In the early afternoon of September 19, 1903, Adirondack land baron Orrando Dexter started down his mile-and-a-half private drive toward Santa Clara. Dexter's carriage wasn't alone on the wooded route that afternoon; his foreman had set out ahead of him, and a stableman followed at a distance. But Dexter was out of sight of both when a gunman—or, possibly, two gunmen—stepped from behind a pile of posts and shot the millionaire in the back. The bullet tore through Dexter and came to rest in his horse's backside; the animal jumped forward, dumping Dexter in the dust. By the time the foreman and stableman arrived on the scene, their employer was already dead. There was no trace of the assassin.

Who would have wanted to murder forty-nine-year-old Dexter, owner of thousands of prime Adirondack acres? Well, just about every local who had ever dealt with him.

Dexter, son of New York City newspaper magnate Henry Dexter, was a fair-weather Adirondacker, spending the inclement months in

Orrando P. Dexter made few friends among his Adirondack neighbors, buying up large tracts of land and then suing anyone who crossed his path. PAINTING BY CHARLES AYER WHIPPLE, COURTESY OF NEW-YORK HISTORICAL SOCIETY, 1906.1

New York City, and maintaining another home in Connecticut. He began buying into the Adirondack dream around 1887, snatching up huge tracts of land in the Franklin County town of Waverly. In the end, he would hold about 7,000 Adirondack acres.

Dexter was an eccentric fellow, spending his free time collecting fancy cats and obsessing over genealogy. He was a licensed attorney who also dabbled in mathematics, publishing *The Division of Angles* in 1881 (through his father's publishing concern, the American News Company). But his very favorite pastime was slapping his neighbors with lawsuits. The *Malone Palladium* dubbed him "the most pertinacious litigant ever known in the courts of Franklin County."

In the untamed Adirondacks, where the concept of private property has always been a bit fuzzy, natives figured they could hunt and fish where they pleased. But Dexter didn't play that way. His land was his, from the tallest tree in his woods to the smallest minnow in his waters. Any and all trespassers would be held accountable. After his murder, the *St. Lawrence Republican* observed that "minor prosecutions against persons who hunted or fished on his domain made Mr. Dexter much disliked by dozens of individuals all over the vicinity."

When Mr. Moneybags wasn't busy protecting his territory, he was griping about his tax bill. Dexter brought a series of actions against the assessors of the town of Waverly, though most sputtered before they reached a courtroom. Then, in January of 1893, one of Dexter's complaints did make it before a judge. In it he argued that his $7,500 assessment was "unequal and erroneous," compared to other local landowners' appraisals. (Never mind that none of his neighbors had anything close to a four-story mansion flanked by a half-dozen outbuildings overlooking a private lake.) Though his case finally appeared in court, Dexter himself didn't. And since he was a no-show, the judge was happy to uphold the assessment. Dexter appealed over and over, failing each time. His parting prize was a bill for the court costs.

Dexter's bitterest battles involved local lumberman Warren Joseph Alfred. There was bad blood almost from the start, since Dexter's land purchases closed off Alfred's best path to market. No other man's logs were going to roll over his land, Dexter decreed, nor float down his streams. To back up his words, Dexter barricaded the egress with downed trees and wire—and brought in a couple of hired guns to patrol his domain. (Though he didn't, according to his lawyer, build a fortified house in the middle of the roadway, as popular legend would have folks believe.)

The blockades didn't faze Alfred; he simply removed them. In the tres-passing suits that followed, Alfred argued the route was a public highway, laid out by the county in 1890. And, according to the *New York Times,* the lumber baron "declared it would take a hundred men with guns to stop him from going across Mr. Dexter's land."

The pair poked at each other in court a bit, and then Alfred took the fight one step further. He had a dam built downstream from his enemy's tract in 1891, causing substantial flooding on Dexter's acres. The dam didn't last—Dexter had it torn down in an eyeblink—but the court battles stemming from its destruction would drag on and on.

Dexter was arrested and briefly held for his dam-busting shenanigans. And that made him mad enough to take his grievances straight to the governor, demanding that the district attorney, H. G. Kilburn, be removed from office. Kilburn was exonerated, but he was not pleased. The D.A. and Dexter were soon trading civil suits.

Meanwhile, Dexter brought a $25,000 claim against the former Sheriff George W. Dustin—incidentally, a co-owner of the land on which Alfred built his inflammatory dam—for malicious prosecution and false impris-onment. Dexter won the battle and lost the war: the judge ruled in his favor, but he refused to award damages. Dexter should have left well enough alone, but he appealed anyway. Dustin won the next round, and Dexter was ordered to cough up some cash.

The ongoing skirmish with Kilburn was settled in November of 1893, though the terms were not reported. The *Malone Palladium* wrote, "Mr. Kilburn is sick, and, being naturally a man of peace, the cases worried him, while Mr. Dexter seems to be happiest when in an ugly law case. He has the habit, too, of appealing his cases when beaten as long as there is an appellate court to go to, and if the suits had been continued it is doubtful if a final determination of them would have been reached in Mr. Kilburn's lifetime."

Dexter never did work or play well with others, but the straw that may have put a hole in the millionaire's back was when he bought up a bunch of land in neighboring St. Lawrence County not long before his murder. The tract included a stream that had always been used by locals to transport pulp wood to the mills. But of course that would never fly with

Dexter, and his no-float policy made one particular mill owner positively apoplectic. After the tragedy, Dexter's lawyer, J. P. Badger, was quick to point out that the man exhibited "intense hostility," though, he added, "Mr. Dexter did not anticipate any such climax to such hostility."

When Dexter was gunned down, there was no shortage of suspects, but not many useful clues. The footprints at the site of the ambush were nondescript—"large and wide," wrote the *Malone Farmer*, "evidently made by a woodsman's or laborer's boot or shoe." The .38-caliber bullet that was removed from the derrière of Dexter's horse was similarly unremarkable, the sort favored by hunters throughout the region.

Dexter's employees offered little information of value. A housekeeper told authorities she heard some nocturnal activity near the house a few days before the killing, and others said they saw a lantern moving around the grounds. Nothing came of those reports, except more speculation. And although only one bullet was found, workers swore that they had heard two shots, one louder than the other, raising the possibility of a second gunman. (Or gunwoman. One of Dexter's newest enemies was his cook, who caused an explosive scene when he fired her a few weeks before.)

The rumors surrounding the search for the murderer were almost as rampant as the rumors concerning the deed itself. The *Malone Farmer* spent a good deal of ink correcting tall tales "concocted to make good reading for gullible city subscribers." No, bloodhounds were not baying through the woods after the dastardly villain. No, St. Regis Mohawks were not trucked in to act as trackers. And was the famous hotelier Paul Smith out leading a pack of searchers? Nope.

Just days after the shooting, the *Plattsburgh Sentinel* reported that "a squad of woodsmen has been sent out to arrest a man suspected of the crime," but the expected collar never happened—and after years of investigation, nobody ever went to the slammer for doing Dexter in. There were a lot of suspects, sure, but also a lot of convincing alibis and not much cooperation around the area. As the *St. Lawrence Republican* pointed out, "Not a few individuals do not mourn much for Mr. Dexter, and if some of them have any idea who is responsible for his assassination they will not aid the authorities."

But Dexter's father loved his son, even if not many others did, and he wasn't about to let the murderer flit away. He started with a $5,000 reward for the capture of the killer, then upped it to $10,000 the following year. Attorney Badger told the *St. Lawrence Republican*, "I have no doubt that unlimited sums will be spent to run this cowardly assassin to earth." He wasn't kidding. For starters, Henry Dexter handed Badger $50,000 worth of American News Company shares.

Orrando Dexter wasn't the only disliked member of the invading class. Alfred Vanderbilt, J. P. Morgan, Seward Webb, William Whitney, William Rockefeller—they all owned obnoxiously large Adirondack spreads. Word was that Rockefeller, who jealously guarded his 52,000 acres, was especially despised. The *St. Lawrence Republican* told readers, "Against several of these men the Adirondack guides have a deadly hatred," and worried that Dexter's unsolved murder could lead to "a reign of terror throughout a wide territory." Other publications poo-pooed the class warfare angle, calling it out as a ploy to pump up circulation. "That there is ill feeling against rich men in the Adirondacks is ridiculous," the *Malone Farmer* scoffed. And Rockefeller continued to visit his wooded wonderland, the *Plattsburgh Sentinel* noted, "with utter disregard for an assassin's bullet."

Henry Dexter searched for his son's killer until his death, in 1910. His healthy reward attracted attention, but no real answers. In 1904, Henry received a letter confessing to the murder: "He put me away from his fishing place and I put him to death." But the untraceable missive was soon discounted. The *Plattsburgh Sentinel* sniffed, "The letter, apparently by design, had been put in an illiterate form to give the appearance of the work of a hunter or back-woodsman." That same year a pack of witnesses was rounded up to testify before the grand jury in Malone, but the panel didn't hear anything juicy enough to indict anyone.

Old Henry Dexter was livid with the lack of progress in the case and published a letter railing against the incompetent natives up north. The *Malone Palladium* didn't think that was very neighborly. They sprang to the defense of their brethren, writing, "We know that the most thorough investigation into all the circumstances . . . was made by the sheriff . . . and that after that investigation was completed a Pinkerton detective, one of the best on the Pinkerton force, reviewed the result and declared that the investigation had been excellent." They also championed the district attorney and the grand jury, who "were reluctantly compelled to admit that the evidence was not sufficient to warrant the finding of an indictment."

Four years later, two more false leads renewed interest in the case. Fred Schmidt, of Colorado, sent Henry a letter outlining a sensational tale—not only did he know who killed Orrando Dexter, he was also there when it happened. His sordid tale went like this: Schmidt worked for a "wealthy and prominent" man who had a falling out with Dexter over a pretty young socialite. So he bushwhacked his rival while Schmidt stood by, then ordered his employee to bury the weapon. This same blackguard got Schmidt's daughter in the family way and paid the pair off to head west, suggesting that they "employ a physician to perform an operation."

Schmidt claimed that he had kept his mouth shut for years because he feared his daughter would be murdered as well. He only came forward now "to be avenged for the ruin of his child"—and to score enough money to move back to New York. It didn't take long for his story to unravel. The most conspicuous red flag was the name of the supposed murderer, a Mr. Jack Chambers, who was easily identified as a work of fiction.

Not long after that whopper hit the papers, a lonely old woman from the Malone area, Mrs. Seymour Jock, alerted authorities that she knew who killed Dexter. But she insisted that she would only tell the Franklin County district attorney the culprit's identity in person. So he trekked out to her homestead to be treated to one of the same tired rumors he had already written off.

A grand jury in Malone took another crack at the case in 1909 with no better luck. It must have been the last straw for Henry Dexter; in October of that year, he took a page from his son's playbook and sued J. P. Badger for the $50,000 bundle he'd handed over at the start of the investigation. Henry died at ninety-eight, still searching for word of his son's assassin, although many suspected the crime was no mystery to the locals. As Alfred L. Donaldson wrote in his 1921 *A History of the Adirondacks*, "it was said that even children knew the murderer's name." ⇥

FURTHER READING

Aber, Ted and Stella King. *The History of Hamilton County.* Lake Pleasant, New York: Great Wilderness Books, 1965.

Bossert, Richard. "Highway Robbery: North River's very own crime of the century." *Adirondack Life.* July/August 2001: 38-42.

Brenan, Dan, ed. *The Adirondack Letters of George Washington Sears, Whose Pen Name Was Nessmuk.* Blue Mountain Lake, New York: The Adirondack Museum, 1962.

Brumley, Charles. *Guides of the Adirondacks: A History.* Utica, New York: North Country Books, 1994.

Clinton Prison at Dannemora. Plattsburgh, New York: Clinton County Historical Museum, 1987.

Connors, Bernard F. *Tailspin: The Strange Case of Major Call.* Latham, New York: British American Publishing, 2002.

DeSormo, Maitland C. *The Heydays of the Adirondacks.* Saranac Lake, New York: Adirondack Yesteryears, Inc., 1974.

Donaldson, Alfred L. *A History of the Adirondacks.* New York: The Century Company, 1921.

Everest, Allan S. *Rum Across the Border: The Prohibition Era in Northern New York.* Syracuse, New York: Syracuse University Press, 1978.

Farnsworth, Cheri L. *Adirondack Enigma: The Depraved Intellect and Mysterious Life of North Country Wife Killer Henry Debosnys.* Charleston, South Carolina: The History Press, 2010.

Gooley, Lawrence P. *Lyon Mountain: The Tragedy of a Mining Town.* Peru, New York: Bloated Toe Enterprises, 2004.

Hearn, Daniel Allen. *Legal Executions in New York State: A Comprehensive Reference, 1639-1963.* Jefferson, North Carolina: McFarland & Company, 1997.

Kudish, Michael. *Railroads of the Adirondacks: A History.* Fleischmanns, New York: Purple Mountain Press, 1996.

Montville, Leigh. *The Mysterious Montague: A True Tale of Hollywood, Golf, and Armed Robbery.* New York: Doubleday, 2008.

O'Brien, Kathryn E. "The Saga of Sam Pasco." *Adirondack Life.* Summer 1976: 8-11+.

O'Brien, Kathryn E. *The Great and the Gracious on Millionaire's Row: Lake George in its Glory.* Sylvan Beach, New York: North Country Books, 1978.

Pearsall, Glenn. *Echoes in these Mountains: Historic Sites and Stories Disappearing in Johnsburg, an Adirondack Community.* Utica, New York: North Country Books, 2008.

Terrie, Philip G. *Contested Terrain: A New History of Nature and People in the Adirondacks.* Syracuse, New York: Syracuse University Press, 1997.

ABOUT THE AUTHOR

Niki Kourofsky holds a bachelor's degree in history, with a concentration in museum studies, and a master's degree in writing and editing. Her Adirondack roots run generations deep, grounded in the ore sand of the one-time mining community of Lyon Mountain. She is a senior editor at *Adirondack Life*, a regional magazine exploring the people, places, and storied history of New York's six-million-acre Adirondack Park. Her hobbies include haphazard parenting, cooking fat-laden regional delicacies, and napping—especially in a pine-shaded camp chair. ⇒⊱

INDEX